"*How Now Shall We Live?* is truly inspiring for those who want to restore to our culture the values that made America great. It reminds us that w : must not only defend what we believe but also inspire others to give witness to the truth alongside us." —**The Honorable Tom DeLay, Majority Whip, United States Senate**

"The singular pleasure that comes from this book is its absolute— learned—refusal to give any quarter to the dogged materialists who deny any possibility that there was a creator around the corner. This is a substantial book, but the reader never tires, as one might from a catechistic marathon. The arguments are cogently and readably presented." —**William F. Buckley in *National Review***

"The newest—and certainly the most important—of Charles Colson's books. . . . The essence of this book is that the Christian faith is not just a theory, not just a system, not just a framework. It is an all-consuming way of life, robustly applicable to every minute of every day of the rest of your life." —**World**

"There is something wrong with the historical development of the evangelical mind . . . a lopsidedness, a prodigious development of one divine gift coupled with the atrophy of another. . . . We know a great deal about saving grace, but next to nothing—though it is one of our doctrines—about common grace. The ambition of Charles Colson and Nancy Pearcey is to do something about this lopsidedness, to strike a blow against the scandal of the evangelical mind. . . . A highly intelligent book, it is not ashamed to speak to ordinary folk." —**First Things**

"*How Now Shall We Live?* is brilliantly lit by its in-depth and succinct diagnosis of the modern mentality . . . an intelligent and thorough-

going critique from a scriptural perspective, of the American/Western culture. . . . The book is a veritable mosaic of precious intellectual gems, artistically designed by Charles Colson and Nancy Pearcey. . . . This book is a virtual 'must' for the thinking Orthodox reader."
—*DOXA, a quarterly review serving the Orthodox Church*

"A magnum opus in the best Schaefferian tradition. It is clearly intended to be . . . a handbook for today's Christian. . . . The authors presuppose that Christianity is more than just a religion of personal salvation: it involves a total world-and-life view." —*Christianity Today*

"A very good and much needed book. . . . Colson argues that Christianity isn't a private faith but a public worldview that, for believers, permeates politics, the arts, education, science and culture." —*Insight*

An "elegantly written tutorial on adopting a biblical worldview and the discipline of thinking Christianly." —*Good News*

"I'd like to recommend a book. It's *How Now Shall We Live?* by Charles Colson, the Watergate guy who got religion while in prison. . . . Now I don't agree with everything Colson says, but the importance of the book is that it raises a question every American ought to face and then answer to his or her own satisfaction: What is your worldview?"
—**Charley Reese, nationally syndicated columnist**

One of "Ten Books Every Preacher Should Read This Year." —*Preaching*

"Deeply troubled by the lack of biblical literacy within the American church, this is Colson's heroic effort to enable believers to accept the importance of having a biblical worldview and devoting themselves to adopting such a life perspective. . . . This book provides a wealth of insight into how we may effectively challenge the post-Christian, post-modern culture in which we live." —*The Barna Report*

"Colson and Pearcey aren't talking about influencing business, politics and culture—they want it transformed through a coherent Christian worldview. Their book will challenge every Christian leader to make an honest assessment about his or her commitment to use leadership gifts in the new millennium to the cause of Christ."
—*Christian Management Report*

"Colson and Pearcey challenge the church to stay on the front lines. Believing that America is on the verge of a great spiritual break-through, the authors want to equip readers to show the world that Christianity is a life system that *works* in every area—family relationships, education, science, and popular culture." —*Virtue*

"A radical challenge to all Christians to understand biblical faith as an entire worldview, a perspective on all of life. Through inspiring teaching and true stories, Colson discusses how to expose the false views and values of modern culture, how to live more fulfilling and satisfying lives in line with the way God created us to live—and more."
—*Youthworker*

(In developing and implementing an organizational learning strategy and integrating it with their organizational practices) "When it came to selecting materials, your *How Now Shall We Live?* was at the top of the list. To our minds this is now the best introduction to a Christian worldview and Christian cultural engagement available in English. At least in our organization, *How Now Shall We Live?* should become an indispensable resource." —*Christian Labour Association of Canada*

1999 Books of the Year - Award of Merit —*Christianity Today*

ANSWERS TO YOUR KIDS' QUESTIONS

HOW NOW SHALL WE LIVE?™

ANSWERS TO YOUR KIDS' QUESTIONS

CHUCK COLSON

Compiled and introduced by
Harold Fickett

Tyndale House Publishers, Inc.
Wheaton, Illinois

Visit Tyndale's exciting Web site at www.tyndale.com

Answers to Your Kids' Questions

Copyright © 2000 by Prison Fellowship Ministries. All rights reserved.

Cover photography copyright © 2000 by James Leland. All rights reserved.

Author photo taken by Russ Busby. All rights reserved.

How Now Shall We Live? is a trademark of Tyndale House Publishers, Inc.

Designed by Justin Ahrens

Edited by Lynn Vanderzalm and Sue Taylor

Unless otherwise indicated, all Scripture quotations are taken from the *Holy Bible,* New International Version® NIV® Copyright © 1973, 1978, 1984 by International Bible Society. Used by permission of Zondervan Publishing House. All rights reserved.

Scripture quotations marked NLT are taken from the *Holy Bible,* New Living Translation, copyright © 1996. Used by permission of Tyndale House Publishers, Inc., Wheaton, Illinois 60189. All rights reserved.

Scripture quotations marked NASB are taken from the *New American Standard Bible,* © 1960, 1962, 1963, 1968, 1971, 1972, 1973, 1975, 1977 by The Lockman Foundation. Used by permission.

Scripture quotations marked "NKJV" are taken from the New King James Version. Copyright © 1979, 1980, 1982 by Thomas Nelson, Inc. Used by permission. All rights reserved.

Scripture quotations marked KJV are taken from the *Holy Bible,* King James Version.

The bulk of the material in this book has been compiled from Chuck Colson's *BreakPoint* radio programs; some content has been taken from speeches and some from previously published books. This material has been compiled and edited into convenient answers for parents to provide their kids to help them live effectively in today's culture.

Library of Congress Cataloging-in-Publication Data

Colson, Charles W.
  Answers to your kids' questions / Chuck Colson with Harold Fickett.
    p. cm.
  ISBN 0-8423-1817-8 (sc)
  1. Christian teenagers—Religious life—Miscellanea. 2. Christian teenagers—Conduct of life—Miscellanea.
I. Fickett, Harold. II. Title.
BV4531.2.C576 2000
  230—dc21   00-041809

Printed in the United States of America

06   05   04   03   02   01   00
8   7   6   5   4   3   2   1

CONTENTS

CHAPTER 3: *Does Modern Science Disprove the Bible and Christianity?*
Science, Evolution, and Intelligent Design . . . **35**

CHAPTER 4: *Can We Really Believe the Bible?*
Reason, Historical Evidence, and the Scriptures . . . **59**

CHAPTER 9: *Should I Keep My Baby?*
Life at the Limits: Pregnancy, Abortion, and Bioethics . . . **139**

CHAPTER 10: *Guess What I Learned Today?*
Schools, Values, and Violence . . . **157**

CHAPTER 11: *What Do I Owe the Government?*
Government, Politics, and Citizenship . . . **175**

CHAPTER 12: *How Can I Be Confident about My Future?*
Work, Career, and Success . . . **191**

A WORD FROM A PARENT OF A TEENAGER

Like many parents, I have a difficult time talking to my teenager, especially about what I most value: my Christian faith. My hesitation is based on assorted grounds, which constantly shift and, like the earth's tectonic plates, clash in earthquake rumblings that shake me to the core.

I like to think my reluctance stems from my teenage son's defensive posturing. The looming expectations of adulthood—that he will be able to earn a living, be the head of a family, find his own distinctive place—daunt him. He reacts by mocking the adult world or by keeping a steel-drum silence that's only one degree stronger, I suspect, than the explosive fear within.

Then there's the matter of when such a discussion might take place. As any parent of a teenager knows, I cannot talk to him any old time I please—not if I want him to respond with something more than suspicion.

Since my son was a toddler, I've learned that our best talks result from completely mysterious changes in the emotional climate. Once, when my son was about four years old, I planned a big outing to the children's zoo in New York's Central Park. I thought of all the fun we would have watching the seals in their habitat as they flopped off high-standing rocks and zoomed, to our pleasure, through the depths of their transparent aquatic tank. I thought of the petting-zoo section, of placing a baby chick in my son's hand and seeing his smile register delight at its fuzzy coat and warm stirring.

The day my son and I went, he had a cold and found all the walking in the chill New York winter more a test of endurance than anything else. We weren't having much fun, and the distance between the day's reality and our hopes made us both glum.

We stopped to have a cup of hot chocolate. When I received change for the snacks, my son asked for a dime. After we sat down, I showed him how to flip his dime, and we started calling heads or tails. This so delighted him that he began to talk to me about his preschool, his friends, and his dawning awareness that kids could sometimes be mean—all things I had asked him about a million times without ever receiving more than a yes, no, or I guess in response.

Nothing much has changed. My best talks with my son still come at odd times, in odd places, and by virtue of spiritual prompts that are impossible to manufacture. For reasons I'm never quite sure of, vistas of inquiry suddenly appear like splayed-out shafts of sunlight.

Talking to any child—much less a teenager—is no easy thing. Sometimes, though, I have taken the risk. I've walked out into those expected vistas of inquiry and invited him to join me.

While running the risk has been worthwhile, I cannot always report happy endings. Indeed, what I've discovered has often been as troubling as I imagined. His thinking, while it hasn't arrived at many firm conclusions, comes at problems or questions from a wholly different direction from my own. I'm finding out how secularized his viewpoint can be.

My son's mind has not been shanghaied by cultists, communists, or other conspiratorial pirates. No one's been out to convert him away from my Christian faith directly.

What rivals my Christian faith as an influence on my son is so pervasive that it's almost as invisible as the air. It's nothing less than our culture's dominant way of thinking, and as such, its expressions are everywhere and endless.

Paradoxically, the ever-present character of this mode of thinking makes it hard to identify sometimes. But here are a few examples:

When Supreme Court Justice Antonin Scalia talked about believing in the resurrection of Jesus Christ, editorialists across the nation laughed at his supernatural beliefs, and some commentators thought such commitments made him unfit to rule on church-and-state questions.

When Congressman Dick Armey said he believed homosexuality was a disordered condition, the president's spokesperson called such beliefs "primitive" even though this belief has always been part of historic Christianity.

Almost every time my son and I watch a movie, we see that if two characters fall in love, they go to bed together. If the movie characters were to worry about whether their sexual relations were sanctioned by marriage, that would be truly peculiar—at this point, almost unprecedented.

All of these developments reflect the dominance of secularism—or naturalistic materialism, to call this way of thinking by its proper philosophical name. Most people in Western society now believe that the world came about by chance. The human race, as the product of chance, must make its own choices and determine its own destiny guided only by whatever collective wisdom it chooses to adopt. The same, the secularists say, applies to individuals. Each person decides what's right for himself or herself. As long as one person's choices don't infringe on someone else's, everyone's choices are equally valid. There is no right and wrong that applies to everybody, not apart from the law, and the law itself is only an expression of majority will. To most people, there is no such thing as a universally valid truth. There is only my truth and your truth and the truth that governments adopt in order to maintain power and, to a lesser degree, the security of the government's citizens.

The conflict between my own Christian faith and this secular faith enters into every important conversation my son and I have. This may sound like an exaggeration, but it's true. Every significant question leads back to where we start from—our answers to the three perennial questions: Who are we? Where do we come from? Where are we going? The way the Christian faith answers those questions differs radically from the answers offered by the secular faith.

For example, my son once asked me what I thought about the fact that the town's mayor was a lesbian and a gay-rights activist. That question led to many more and described the boundaries between my worldview and the one my son encounters almost every waking moment of every day.

I started the conversation by saying that while I thought the mayor had real administrative abilities, I believed her understanding of sexuality to be mistaken and that inevitably her private choices about sexual activity would form her character in a way that would have public consequences.

But she couldn't help being a lesbian, he said. She had a right to lead her private life the way she wanted to.

We quickly agreed that the issue came down to compassion. Was it more compassionate to accept this woman's homosexuality, or was it more compassionate to warn her against the dangers of her homosexuality? Were there dangers? If so, what were they?

I saw that to explain my point of view to my son, I had to begin with very basic questions. I tried to show him that we would answer the question differently depending on how we thought the world came into being. Did God create the world, or did it come about by chance? If God created the world, then God created people and knew what was best for them.

If the world came about by chance, then heterosexuality and homosexuality have only the meanings we give them. We might see them as equally good or bad depending on how we decide to look at them.

I told my son once again that I believe God created us, knew what was best for us, and in the Bible revealed the best way for us to live.

That opened up questions about the reliability of the Scriptures, what exactly they say about God's character, how Jesus fits in, and so forth. We started talking about the cause of a gay-rights activist and ended up talking about . . . well, everything.

I'm sure every parent can remember a similar incident, in which a TV show, a pop song, a news item, or a development at school opened up a question that quickly led to many others.

Chuck Colson has spent decades answering just such questions, with a particular gift for grounding his answers in the bedrock of Christian faith. He knows how to trace the lines of argument back to their foundations. He is also a tremendous storyteller, using incidents from today's world to address issues of ultimate concern.

This book presents Chuck Colson's thinking in a question-and-answer format to help parents—as well as educators and youth workers—answer their teenagers' questions and put their Christian faith at the heart of their parenting and teaching. The questions gathered here have been phrased as teenagers might ask them. They have also been grouped in subject areas (God, the Bible, science and evolution, etc.), with one answer building to some degree on the one before. The one hundred questions and answers here, although hardly exhaustive of everything a teenager might ask a parent or teacher or youth worker, cover the truly important differences between a Christian way of looking at life and the secular outlook.

The book can be (and will be, I expect) used in a variety of ways. You might begin preparing for the talks you would really like to have with your teenagers by reading through all of the sections. I suggest tackling one section at a sitting, focusing on the checklist of key points at the end of each section. You will notice that the big-picture questions are addressed first because the answers to those questions form the foundations to the answers about the more urgent questions your teenager may have about contemporary issues.

You might also use the book as a supplement to daily devotions, reading one question and answer a day and praying about how the answer might address problems you are having with your teen. Even the most abstract discussions have some application in this way. For example, God's role in creation means that we can trust God to know what's best for us, and archaeological evidence for the reliability of Scripture reinforces the Bible's ability to speak to issues such as sexual morality and other topical concerns.

You can also turn to the book as a reference when a particular question comes up. The table of contents lists all of the questions answered so that you can find them at a glance. I imagine your copy will be well thumbed all through your child's teenage years.

Also, while this book is intended chiefly for parents, teenagers can read it for themselves. When a question comes up, you and your teenager might read the appropriate question and answer together as a means of continuing your own discussion. You may find yourselves tracing through much of the helpful, informative, and, at times, humorous material gathered here.

I know how hard it is to talk with my own teenager, and I'm grateful for the help I've received through reading Chuck Colson's reflections on life's truly important questions. The apostle Paul charges us to be ready to give an account of our faith to anyone who asks—an admonition a parent can't help but take to heart.

We know the responsibility we have, but we need resources to address that daunting task. This book will be an invaluable tool.

If you find that you would like to explore more fully the worldview issues discussed in this book, I recommend that you read Colson's legacy book, *How Now Shall We Live?* In this profound book he explores how the Christian worldview addresses the many opposing worldviews that our teenagers—and we—confront every day, and how we can live out our Christianity and transform our culture. If your teenager wishes to explore some of these issues, he or she may want to read the soon-to-be-released student edition of *How Now Shall We Live?*

HAROLD FICKETT

A WORD FROM CHUCK COLSON

Harold Fickett, who collaborated with me on this book, has shared with you why this book is important to him as the father of a teenager. He is not alone. Many people have been asking for this kind of book.

It started a few years ago when several people from different walks of life challenged me to do something—and whenever that happens, I stop and listen because I suspect God may be trying to get my attention.

The first person was the woman in charge of education in my own church. "What can I tell my daughter when she brings all these tough questions home from school?" she asked. "Can you please give me the information I need so I can protect her from the assaults on her faith she encounters every day in school?"

Another challenge came from a woman who approached me when I was traveling on a plane. "Mr. Colson," she said, "you give us wonderful apologetics material on your radio program, *BreakPoint*. Could you put it all together by category and give us something we could use to teach our kids—to keep them from being taken in by the false ideas they're getting from the culture?"

Finally, on a trip to Scotland some Christian friends who run an excellent publishing company there challenged me to write an apologetics book that would help parents teach their kids the basic truths of a biblical worldview.

That was it. It seemed clear that I was being called to take my articles and the *BreakPoint* scripts and shape the material into a form that parents can use to help train their children to see all of life from a biblical worldview. For that matter the material is useful to all of us—

grandparents, youth pastors, and counselors alike—who have to answer the questions young people are asking.

This information is something young people are eager to have. Teenagers growing up in Christian families today are acutely aware that their faith is under attack as never before—even in officially sanctioned arenas like the public schools. Consider the recent controversy over the Kansas education standards. The state board of education merely stood up against the aggressive nationalizing of science standards, which showcased naturalistic evolution in a more dogmatic way than ever. The board decided to give local schools a choice about whether or not they would teach the broad, speculative aspects of evolution. But dozens of hysterical editorials decried the vote as religious prejudice and accused the board of pandering to the Religious Right and banning science from the classroom.

But what happens when schools become evangelists for naturalism, the idea that we came from a blind, random process? One of my colleagues at Prison Fellowship found out. One day her six-year-old son came home from his first-grade class and asked, "Mom, who's lying—you or my teacher?" His mother had taught him that a loving God created him for a purpose. But his teacher said just the opposite—that he was the product of an impersonal, uncaring evolutionary process. This young boy had wisely concluded that both philosophies could not be true, and he was struggling to determine which one he should accept—in first grade!

It goes without saying that the Christian worldview is under even more relentless attack in the popular culture—on television and in movie theaters. Television programs like *Dawson's Creek* teach teens that they are little more than bundles of raging hormones. The film *Pleasantville* carried a blatant message that unrestrained sexual indulgence leads to increased health, creativity, intelligence, and inner peace. (There was not a word about the real history of the sexual revolution, which has brought us AIDS, skyrocketing divorce rates, unwanted pregnancies, and all the other social ills that have followed.)

Parents can't even let their guard down on vacation. If you take your kids to Disney's Epcot Center in Florida or to the Smithsonian

Institution in Washington, D.C., they will see colorful and engaging displays, all teaching evolution as fact. Not a hint about contrary evidence or about the scientific disputes that are today undermining standard Darwinian theory.

Walk down the street to the art museum, and the attack on Christianity is even more outrageous. In the highbrow culture of the arts, it is fashionable to thumb one's nose at traditional religion and morality. From ancient times until our own century, the art world accepted the Christian view that art is a way of representing transcendent ideals such as truth, goodness, and beauty. But not anymore. A recent exhibit at the Brooklyn Museum of Art in New York featured a portrait of the Virgin Mary smeared with elephant feces and surrounded by photographs of human sexual organs. Art has been reduced to a political tool aimed at shocking the sensibilities of the middle class.

If we are going to train up children who have the resources to enter the cultural warfare, we parents must learn to apply the Christian worldview to every aspect of our life. We can't give our children what we don't have ourselves.

This takes wisdom and discernment, as I recently discovered myself. One day my wife, Patty, came home from a Bible study with a story from one of the mothers there. The woman's thirteen-year-old son had received a low grade for giving a wrong answer on his weekly quiz in earth science class. In reply to the question "Where did Earth come from?" Tim had written, "God created it." His test came back with a big red check and twenty points marked off his grade. The "correct" answer, according to the teacher, was that Earth is the product of the big bang.

The women in Patty's Bible study urged Tim's mother to march into the classroom and show the teacher what the Bible says. "It's right there in Genesis 1," they said. "God created the heavens and the earth."

But as soon as Patty told me the story, I reached for the phone to call Tim's mother. "Don't go to the teacher and read Genesis," I cautioned.

She was taken aback. "But the Bible says—"

"As believers, we know that Scripture is inspired and authoritative," I explained, "but Tim's teacher will dismiss it out of hand. She'll say, 'That's religion. I teach science.' What you need to do is bring in the scientific evidence showing that the big bang idea actually supports Christianity."

In science class we ought to raise questions such as, What came before the big bang? What caused it? If the big bang was the origin of the universe itself, then its cause must be something *outside* the universe. The truth is that the big bang theory gives dramatic support to the biblical teaching that the universe had a beginning—that space, matter, and time itself are finite. Far from challenging the Christian faith, as Tim's teacher seemed to think, the theory actually gives startling evidence *for* the faith.

In such situations we need to avoid giving the mistaken idea that Christianity is opposed to science. If we are too quick to quote the Bible, we will never break out of the common negative stereotype of Christians—especially the caricature of believers as mindless dogmatists from the play *Inherit the Wind*. We should not oppose science with religion; we should oppose bad science with better science.

It might help to remember that we are not the only generation to worry that the surrounding culture is corrupting our children. It may surprise you to learn that America was first settled by people who were concerned about their kids. Before the English-born Pilgrims ever came to the New World, they had *already* achieved religious freedom—by immigrating to Holland. But they pulled up stakes once more, in large part because they were disturbed about the effect Dutch culture was having on their children. As Pilgrim father William Bradford records in his diary, their teenagers were influenced by the "great licentiousness of youth in that countrie" and were drawn away by evil examples. Some were leaving their families and living dissolute lives, "to the great grief of their parents and dishonor of God." Under the circumstances, immigrating to America—a country free from Europe's corrupting influences—seemed like the best solution.

Most of us don't have the luxury of packing up our kids and finding an untouched wilderness to live in. That's why I've put together this book—to help you look at today's toughest questions from a consistently Christian perspective.

Use it as after-dinner reading with your children around the table. Take a few questions and answers and work through them, helping your kids understand the issues. Or read a question at breakfast and discuss the answer as you drive your kids to school. Or consult the list of questions in the table of contents when your teenager poses an unexpected tough question.

The Old Testament commands us not only to impress God's words on our hearts and souls; we're also told, "Teach them to your children, talking about them when you sit at home and when you walk along the road, when you lie down and when you get up" (Deut. 11:19). In modern lingo, that might include when you are taking them to soccer practice, watching a video, or sharing a pizza together.

It is my prayer that this book will give believing parents the tools they need to bring up a new generation of young people with biblically trained minds, capable of creating a genuinely Christian culture.

CHUCK COLSON
Washington, D.C.

PART 1
FAITH AND THE BIG
QUESTIONS

CHAPTER 1

Does God Exist, and Can We Know Him?
God and Contemporary Thinking

Q 1: *Does life really have any meaning? Sometimes everything seems so pointless.*

This question can be so disturbing, particularly when our own kids ask it, that we respond by wishing it away. "You don't mean that," we say, effectively stopping an important conversation before it starts. We sense it will take us rapidly into areas where we are in over our head.

Parents aren't the only ones who have trouble with this question. When President Clinton went before an MTV audience, the atmosphere turned serious as an eighteen-year-old girl named Dahlia Schweitzer stood up and said, "It seems to me that [singer] Kurt Cobain's recent suicide exemplified the emptiness that many in our generation feel. How do you propose to . . . teach our youth how important life is?"

What a great question. With breathtaking suddenness this teenage girl raised one of the most profound issues of human existence.

President Clinton hedged for a moment. The *New York Times* commented, tongue in cheek, that the president did not seem to have a legislative answer for this problem. I should hope not! Life's deepest questions cannot be addressed by passing a meaning-of-life bill.

But the president did not seem to have any *other* kind of answer either. His response was couched in the touchy-feely language characteristic of our therapeutic culture. We don't really have to know life's meaning, he suggested; we just have to learn how to feel good about ourselves.

What young people really need, the president said, is improved self-esteem—the feeling that "they are the most important person in the world to somebody." He told kids to avoid suicide by remembering that, after all, "there can always be a better tomorrow," a line apparently paraphrased from Scarlett O'Hara in *Gone with the Wind*.

But the meaning of life cannot be reduced to feeling good. After all, Kurt Cobain used drugs to feel better. Obviously it wasn't enough. In fact, what both Cobain's death and Dahlia's question tell us is that a therapeutic culture fails to satisfy our deepest yearnings.

So when our teenagers ask this question sincerely, they deserve our full attention. Asking the question may be the beginning of a true religious quest. If our teenagers have been brought up in the church—even if they have accepted Christ as their personal Lord and Savior—this question may still be part of their growth in spiritual understanding.

No one—man or woman, boy or girl—can live for long without a sense of purpose, without an understanding of life's ultimate meaning. Let me tell you a story about the lengths (or heights) to which people will go in order to invent a meaning for themselves when they sense life has none.

Larry Walters was a thirty-three-year-old truck driver who lived in a small development of tract homes in Los Angeles just beyond the L.A. airport. Every Saturday afternoon he would sit in a lawn chair in his small, chain-link-fenced backyard, sunning himself and drinking a six-pack.

The boredom—or purposelessness—of the situation drove Larry to try something novel. He came up with the idea (I suspect after a second six-pack) of attaching some balloons to his lawn chair and floating up about one hundred feet in the air, drifting over his neighbors' backyards and waving at them. He went out and bought forty-five hot-air weather balloons, had them inflated with helium, and brought them back to his house.

Larry's neighbors came over to watch and helped him hold down the chair as he attached the forty-five balloons. He armed himself with a BB gun so that if he went too high, he could shoot out a few balloons and keep from rising more than one hundred feet above the

ground. He also equipped himself with peanut butter and jelly sand-
wiches and another six-pack.

Then he was ready. He shouted to his neighbors, "Let go!"

They did, but he didn't rise one hundred feet; he went up eleven
thousand feet! He never shot out even one of the balloons because he
was too busy clutching the chair! He was first spotted by a Continental
Airlines captain who reported that someone in a lawn chair had just
gone by his DC10. (The captain was asked to report immediately to the
tower when he landed.) For four hours (this is a true story!) Los Angeles
International Airport diverted flights coming in because Larry Walters
was hanging on to his lawn chair at eleven thousand feet.

The authorities sent up helicopters and all sorts of rescue aircraft
and eventually guided him back to the ground. When Larry landed at
dusk (I remember seeing all this on television), it was an extraordinary
scene. There were sirens, police cars with their bubble lights spinning,
and hordes of camera crews converging on this man as he landed in
his lawn chair.

They shoved a microphone in his face and asked, "Were you scared?"

His eyes were as big as saucers. "Yep."

"Are you going to do it again?"

"Nope."

"Why did you do it in the first place?"

Larry Walters replied, "You can't just sit there."

Something within us tells us there has to be more to life than mindless relaxation. Something within us drives us to find life's meaning—
or to go to extraordinary lengths to create our own.

You can't just sit there.

Human beings cannot live without a sense of purpose. Scripture
teaches that we were made to know God and to return God's love—
that's the sum and substance of every person's reason for living. Made
in God's image (Gen. 1:26-27), we sense this truth about ourselves
even when we cannot explain it clearly. Our built-in sense of purpose
is so strong that when people turn away from God, they will turn to
something else in order to make sense out of their lives, to define
some purpose for their existence (Rom. 1:18-22).

The earliest chapters of Genesis set forth this purpose and extend its meaning into our work and daily activities. We are to cultivate the earth, to name the animals (as we do even today in discovering new species), to exercise dominion, becoming cocreators (or partners) with God in caring for the earth's resources. Our work actually furthers God's great creative purpose. When we do our work well, it reflects God's glory and gives him praise. God's purpose can sustain us in triumph or tragedy, in despair and disappointment, and in moments of great joy. Our life and work indeed have purpose: to bring glory to God.

So when your teenager asks, "Does life really have any meaning?" answer, "Yes! To know God and return his love!" (or, in the words of the *Westminster Shorter Catechism*, to "glorify God and enjoy him forever"). And then go on to discuss how this gives purpose to the young person's life in the present.

You made us for yourself, and our hearts find no peace until they rest in you.

Saint Augustine, *Confessions*

For example: Has he or she just broken up with a girlfriend or boyfriend? (Such an event often provokes this question.) Talk together about how relationships aid or hinder our relationship with God. What purpose do they have in the larger scheme of things? For relationships—like everything else—can assume their appropriate meanings once we understand our ultimate reason for living. If we don't understand humankind's ultimate purpose, the meaning of our lesser purposes will always become distorted and assume either too much or too little significance.

Q 2: *But how can I know and love a God I'm not sure exists? Is there really a God?*

This is a huge question, and we can approach it in several ways. First, the Scriptures teach that God has revealed himself so clearly that only fools deny his existence (Ps. 14:1; Rom. 1:20). Then the Bible says that we can discover God's reality through (1) the testimony of creation and (2) the witness of conscience—for we are made in the image of God.

In the book of Romans the apostle Paul writes, "From the time the world was created, people have seen the earth and sky and all that God made. They can clearly see his invisible qualities—his eternal power and divine nature. So they [people who are in rebellion against God] have no excuse whatsoever for not knowing God" (Rom. 1:20, NLT).

The entire Bible, both Old and New Testaments, echoes Paul's argument, which in philosophical terms is known as the argument from design. "The heavens declare the glory of God," the psalmist writes (Ps. 19:1). And Christ asks us to consider how God cares for the sparrows and the lilies of the field. What we see testifies to what we cannot see.

The apostle Paul also writes in this same passage: "The truth about God is known to them instinctively. God has put this knowledge in their hearts [again, referring to people who have turned away from God]. . . . Yes, they knew God, but they wouldn't worship him as God or even give him thanks. And they began to think up foolish ideas of what God was like. The result was that their minds became dark and confused" (Rom. 1:19-21, NLT).

Paul alludes here to a foundational scriptural notion that goes back to Genesis. The human person is made in the image of God. In other words, when God created us, he made us to be mirror images of himself; we are creatures who resemble our Creator in distinctive ways. We have free choice; we are creatures of reason; we are creative; we are made for meaningful work; we are meant to exist in relationship—in all these ways and others we are made in God's image. For this reason we sense, without being taught, that there must be a God.

Don Richardson, a Canadian missionary, spent several years studying the beliefs of different cultures. He discovered that all of the ancient tribes of history believed in the existence of a supreme being. This belief assumed various forms, but belief in some type of god was universal. He also discovered many stories of people journeying from isolated locations to hear a missionary preach. When they heard the gospel of Christ for the first time, they would say, "That is the One [meaning God] I have been wanting to know about."

One of the best stories showing that the truth of God is evident within us is told in my book *The Body*. It is the story of my friend Irina Ratushinskaya. Irina, a Soviet dissident imprisoned for five years in the Gulag, mentally wrote and memorized three hundred poems, which were published to worldwide acclaim upon her release. Her autobiographical *Grey Is the Color of Hope* details her life and imprisonment.

Irina's parents and schoolteachers were atheists. When Irina was nine years old, after listening to atheistic teaching from her teachers and her family, she figured, *My parents told me there aren't any ghosts. They told me there aren't any goblins. They only told me those things once, though. They tell me there isn't a God every week. There must be a God.* In other words, if there weren't something to it, they wouldn't be fighting so hard against it.

She started to read the great Russian authors Pushkin and Tolstoy and Dostoyevsky, whose writings contain much of the gospel. Irina became a believer because of this great literature.

Years later when she was in prison, the authorities tried to freeze her to death. She was huddled up against a wall, shuddering with cold, when she had an incredible sense that people around the world were praying for her. It was true. A group praying for Christians in prison had an extensive prayer chain for Irina—I was part of it—and somehow she knew it.

Whether in the worst of circumstances or even in cultures that have not been evangelized, people know there is a God. My own memories teach me this. Long before my conversion, when I attended church only occasionally and it didn't mean anything to me, I went sailing one day with my six-year-old son. I can remember saying, "Thank you, God, for giving me this son." I didn't know who God was, but something within me declared I should be grateful to him for my child.

Just before Bertrand Russell—an avowed atheist and author of *Why I Am Not a Christian*—died, he sent a letter to a friend. He wrote in his autobiography, "Something in one seems obstinately to belong to God, and to refuse to enter into any earthly communion—at least that is how I should express it if I thought there was a god. It is odd, isn't it? I care passionately for this world and many things and people in it, and yet . . . what is it all? There *must* be something more important, one feels, though I don't believe there is."

God is there. We know it even if we are in rebellion.

The inherent truth that God's existence is evident to everyone reveals itself especially through conscience—one of the most profound ways in which the image of God in us testifies to our Creator. The apostle Paul refers to this as the works of God's law written on our hearts, which justify or condemn our particular behaviors (Rom. 2:14-15).

Five or six years ago a teacher asked fifteen students in a class, "If a one-thousand-dollar bill is lying on the ground and someone comes along and picks it up and turns it in, did that person do the right thing?" The students answered yes. The teacher questioned further. "Let's say you are hungry and have hungry children and you find that one thousand dollars and yet you turn it in. Did you do the right thing?" Still the students answered yes. "What if you know that it was dropped by a drug dealer who had gotten it in an illegal drug transaction. Is it still the right thing?" It still is.

How do we know this?

C. S. Lewis, an Oxford scholar, was one of the great intellectuals of the twentieth century. An atheist who set out to prove that there was no God, Lewis instead became a deeply professing Christian. In his book *Mere Christianity* he says that a sense of right and wrong, a sense of "oughtness," is universal. Where does this sense come from? Lewis argues that it doesn't come from biology or genetics or psychology. It comes from God—the image of God in which we are made.

Lewis uses the term *Tao,* a word taken from Eastern religion, to sum up this inherent and universal human sense of right and wrong. He shows that the universal phenomenon of conscience proves there must be a Lawgiver, a God who gives us this unaccountable understanding.

So when your kids raise the question of whether or not God exists, help them to see that the evidence of history and the conclusions of great minds concur with what creation and conscience declare: Yes, God exists, without a doubt.

Q 3: But what if people created God out of their own need to feel cared for?

Sometimes our kids say to us, "Don't talk to me about the Bible. Of course the Bible says there's a God. But what if he's just a creation based on people's own needs?" If your kids have picked up on this objection to God's existence, they have been influenced by a strong intellectual current that's been around for the last two hundred years.

The influential German philosopher Ludwig Feuerbach believed that God was made in the image of man, that God was a creation of the human mind. So did Sigmund Freud, who wrote, "A theological dogma might be refuted [to a person] a thousand times, provided, however, he had need of it, he again and again accepts it as true."

Is religion then just a psychological prop? Is it merely a crutch for the weak?

Consider the nature and character of the God revealed in the Bible. If we were making up our own god, does it make sense that we would create one with such harsh demands for justice, righteousness, service, and self-sacrifice as we find in the biblical texts? Would the members of the pious New Testament religious establishment have created a God who condemned them for their own hypocrisy? Would even a zealous disciple have invented a Messiah who called his followers to sell all, give their possessions to the poor, and follow him to their death? The skeptic who believes that the Bible's human authors manufactured their God out of psychological need has not read the Scriptures carefully. That skeptic may have penetrated to the heart of New Age religion, but he or she has not understood the teaching of the Bible.

If we were going to invent a god to prop up our spirits, we wouldn't create one who asked Mother Teresa to spend her life picking dying people out of Calcutta gutters just so they might die with dignity, knowing they were loved.

We would invent the god of superstition—the god who forecasts our future and can be persuaded (or bribed) through prayer or chanting or séances to do our own bidding, a god who never condemns but only condones our most selfish inclinations and desires. We'd invent the god of the New Age.

But the God of the Judeo-Christian tradition is a God who demands everything from us—most of all that we confront, not flee from, reality.

Q 4: *Why does the universe exist?*

Ultimately this question also deals with God's existence. The popular theologian and apologist Francis Schaeffer used to say it's the first question: Why is there something rather than nothing? Why is there anything at all?

Through the centuries people have attempted to answer this question. Astonishingly, the deepest thinkers in all of human history have been able to come up with only four possible answers. As difficult as this question may be, there are only a limited number of possible replies:

First, the universe is an illusion. That is, we are not here. What we see out there is simply a giant picture that somebody has painted on a screen. It isn't there. It's only an idea in one's mind, just as you or I may be only an idea in someone else's mind.

Second, the universe is self-created. That is, the universe generated itself. First there was nothing, and then nothing became everything.

Third, the universe is preexisting, eternal. This is the dominant view today in all quarters. Carl Sagan, in his video series and book *Cosmos*, became famous teaching that the cosmos "is all there is or ever will be." That's it! The cosmos. (Incidentally, this is why so many people are turning to earth worship. If the universe has always been there, then it is entitled to some status as our god on the basis of its eternity.)

Fourth, a preexisting and eternal force outside the universe or the cosmos—namely God—brought the cosmos into being.

The first answer, that the universe is an illusion, may be an interesting philosophical conjecture, but no one but philosophers—who allow themselves to suspend their own sense of living in space and time for the sake of argument—has ever considered it seriously. As a blueprint for meaningful existence, the notion of creation as illusion is eminently unworkable.

In the Enlightenment era, two centuries ago in France, a group of thinkers called the Encyclopedists—Diderot and D'Alembert being principal among them—came up with the second answer, the notion that the universe simply created itself. There are two problems with this idea.

The law of causality argues that something that exists presupposes a force that brought it into existence. If we stumble upon a house in the middle of a field, we are sure that at some point in time one or more people built it.

Another problem with this idea, an even more important objection, stems from the "law of noncontradiction." This law states that an orange cannot be both an orange and a steel girder at the same time. It also cannot be itself and its own cause—both a house, for example, and the builder of the house. For the Encyclopedists to be right, the universe would have to be not only itself but also the force that brought it into being—two different things—and at the same time. So most people eventually discarded this theory.

Some still argue that in the midst of nothingness—before the universe came into existence—chance created the something that became everything. So chance, a property that still belongs to the universe, according to these thinkers, brought about what it then became a part of. But how? This theory demands that we credit a purely mathematical concept with godlike capacities. It solves nothing (and requires more faith than the biblical view!).

Most people today have disposed of this notion and believe the third answer—that the cosmos, everything that you can see, is all that there is or ever will be: The cosmos is eternal. However, this belief creates another major problem. I call it an intellectual cop-out. Because many people are unwilling to acknowledge that there had to be some first cause, they insist that what we see is all we can know. But the character of the universe itself argues against this.

To say that the universe is eternal and preexisting might be possible if within the universe we could find anything that was eternal. There is nothing in the universe (except perhaps in the area of quantum physics in which we are still investigating the motion of molecules) that is not contingent, that is not dependent on something else.

During Carl Sagan's lifetime he used to answer this objection by saying that the whole can be greater than the sum of the parts.

Yes, of course, the whole can be greater than the sum of the parts, but it can't be of a different character. This is a fundamental intellectual flaw in Sagan's argument—the dominant argument of unbelievers today. There is nothing in the universe that is preexisting and eternal. The universe declares its dependence on something or someone else.

The most reasonable answer turns out to be the fourth one: The universe exists because a preexistent, eternal being—God—created it. People didn't make up God; God created the world and us too.

Do these arguments then prove God's existence? Not in the way mathematical formulas can prove 2 + 2 = 4. But they do show that God's existence is the most reasonable assumption—especially when compared with the alternative.

The reasonableness of God's existence can't be equated with knowing God. But the best arguments on this subject may motivate us to spend our life seeking to "glorify God and enjoy him forever." Your kids may be encouraged in their seeking to know that belief in God is neither irrational nor out-of-date. And this can help to keep them active in the quest to know him.

Q 5: *So who created God?*

Have you heard this comeback from a teenager? It's worth comment because it introduces another argument that addresses God's existence and what makes him who he is.

An eleventh-century clergyman named Anselm of Canterbury said: "God is that [being], the greater than which cannot be conceived." This is called the ontological argument for the existence of God—that is, an argument about the kinds of things that exist. If we cannot conceive of anyone or anything greater than God, then nothing and no one could have created him because that creator would have to be something even greater. The idea of God is the logical end of our speculations.

The early seventeenth-century philosopher Descartes, who was an influential figure at the beginning of the Age of Reason, expanded on this argument by saying that the very idea of God could come only from God because we couldn't conceive of a God if God didn't give us the ability to do so.

Perhaps the best way to understand this argument is to look at its flip side. Jonathan Edwards, the first president of Princeton and one of the greatest intellects ever produced in the Western world, preferred the flip side of the argument; he said one cannot conceive of nothingness. "Nothingness is what sleeping rocks dream about," Edwards wrote. In other words, the inescapable fact of existence forces us to consider where everything came from, and this, as we have seen, leads us by turns to God.

If you want my formulation, it is simply this: We humans cannot conceive of nonexistence. The highest thing we can conceive of is God. We may not know God yet, but we know that he is there. Because we exist, we realize (because the law of causality is such a universal law) that we can't exist unless something or someone has brought us into existence.

Q 6: Why doesn't God show himself more clearly?

During a question-and-answer period after I had given a speech at a university, a philosophy professor stood up and said, "If your God exists, I, as an atheist, would be convinced if you could ask him to perform a miracle at this moment."

In response, I said two things. First, I referred to Jesus' wilderness temptation. "If you are the Son of God," Satan said, "throw yourself down" from the highest roof of the temple, so the angels will save you. Jesus replied: "Do not put the Lord your God to the test" (Matt. 4:5-

7). God does not need to perform miracles to validate his witnesses or prove himself to anyone. He is not under our command; if he were, he would not be much of a God—one who had to jump and perform whenever we demanded.

But I went on to say that if the man really wanted to see a miracle, all he had to do was look at me. If someone really knew what had been in my heart before my conversion, he would have to say, "Here stands a miracle." And millions of believers from every age and walk of life could tell a similar story of transformation.

People in every age pose the same question: Why doesn't God prove that he exists through some powerful demonstration? In Jesus' day, the Jews expected the Messiah to appear as a king surrounded by soldiers in glinting armor and mounted on horses.

But every Christmas season God reminds us what *his* answer to that question is: His transforming power appears in ways that confound our expectations, just as his Son, Jesus Christ, came not as a crowned king but as a frail baby in a smelly stable, among the common folk. He came quietly—born in the most out-of-the-way place and laid in a manger—not with trumpets or banner headlines but in all simplicity, so as to fully empty himself of his glory as God's own Son. Later in his life Jesus would perform many miracles as signs of his mission, but the greatest miracle of all was his willingness to give up the glories of heaven and identify completely with his creatures, alienated by sin. C. S. Lewis puts it this way: "The central miracle asserted by Christians is the Incarnation. They say that God became Man. Every other miracle prepares for this, or exhibits this, or results from this."

When God became human, he found the perfect means to invite humankind back into relationship with himself. When God appears to everyone at the consummation of history, people will have no choice but to believe. Until then, God has chosen to respect human freedom by offering an invitation that isn't shadowed by coercion—the overpowering force of a revelation that would leave us all cowering in submission. No, he chooses to use the "foolish things" of the world—the obscure, the poor, the marginal—to confound the wise (1 Cor. 1:27). God does not show himself more clearly because of his love. Because he wants us to choose to love him, he preserves our capacity for faith or faithlessness by offering a sufficient and complete revelation in Christ rather than by giving a coercive demonstration of his power.

Q 7: *If everything you say is true, why don't more people believe?*

Our democratic society can sometimes lead children to believe that truth is the result of popular opinion; if something isn't popular, it can't be true. When answering this question, we need to start by showing that truth often runs counter to popular opinion. For example, the world appears to be flat, but in fact it's round. So what seems right to a lot of people—in this case, the whole world before Copernicus—isn't always so.

Atheism, or the refusal to believe in God, is almost always based on moral objections to the existence of God. During the last twenty years I have found some people with intellectual objections, but not many. Most objections are moral.

> *Only fools say in their hearts, "There is no God.". . . The Lord looks down from heaven on the entire human race; he looks to see if there is even one with real understanding, one who seeks for God.*
>
> Psalm 14:1-2, NLT

Mortimer Adler—philosopher, cofounder of the Great Books series, and arguably one of the great minds of our time—was pressed to become a Christian late in life. He was born Jewish, and he admitted being "on the edge of becoming a Christian several times." Why didn't he convert? He wrote: "If one converts by a clear conscious act of will, one had better be prepared to live a truly Christian life. So you ask yourself, 'Are you prepared to give up all of your vices and weaknesses of the flesh?'" It took Adler a long time to feel he was prepared. He experienced the great gulf between the mind and the heart. Adler went through an incredible agony because intellectually he knew there was a God, but morally he was unwilling to take up the demands of Christianity. Six years after he wrote in such a hesitant manner, he gave his life to Christ and is today a professing Christian. He realized that the truth of God is more important than our moral objections. I have run into hundreds, maybe thousands, of people like Mortimer Adler.

Once I debated Madalyn Murray O'Hair, the famous atheist. It was a fascinating experience because she was so vicious, even when the debate was over. I tried to talk to her nicely. I couldn't get her to respond in kind. "Tell me," I said, "why are you fighting so hard against something that, as you see it, doesn't exist? Why are you so angry about it? I don't understand it."

Actually, I do understand it because such animosity represents moral rebellion against God. And that rebellion is a fight to the death—the death of one's own willfulness.

Young people today are under great pressure—from peers and from the popular culture—to throw off every moral restraint and do whatever they feel like doing. For many teenagers, accepting the existence of God and doing battle with the daily pressures coming at them is a great struggle. Rebellion is much easier. But we have to subdue that rebellion, a task that can take a lifetime and be completed only by God's grace.

KEY POINTS IN BRIEF

✓ We were created to know God, to return God's love, and to enjoy communion with God. That's the meaning of life.

✓ We were created in God's image.

✓ When people turn away from God, they feel compelled to turn to something else to define their purpose for existence.

✓ The Bible says we can discover God's reality through (1) the testimony of creation and (2) the witness of conscience.

✓ The God of the Bible demands too much ever to be considered a crutch. He calls us to moral perfection and self-sacrifice.

✓ The god of superstition—who also happens to be the god of the New Age belief system—is the kind of god we would invent: a god who never condemns but only condones our most selfish inclinations and desires.

✓ The universe exists because a preexistent, eternal being, God, created it. This is the most reasonable explanation as well as the witness of Christianity.

✓ God reveals himself to us in ways that do not compromise human freedom. He often demonstrates his transforming power in ways that confound our expectations, as he did in the incarnation of his Son, Jesus Christ.

✓ Atheism is almost always based on moral objections to the existence of God.

CHAPTER 2

If God Is Good, Why Is There Evil?
The Problem of Evil, Sin,
and God's Love for Humankind

Q 8: *Did God create evil?*

The toughest intellectual barrier to Christian faith is not, as many believe, whether God created the world. The greatest scientist of this century, Albert Einstein—*Time* magazine's Person of the Century—saw clearly that the universe is designed and orderly and that it therefore must be the result of a mind, not merely of matter bumping around randomly in space. As Einstein put it, the order of the universe "reveals an intelligence of such superiority" that it overshadows all human intelligence.

What stymied Einstein was something much tougher: the question of suffering and evil. Knowing there was a designer, he agonized over the character of this designer: How could God be good and yet allow the terrible things that befall mankind?

The problem of evil can be stated simply: If God is both all-good and all-powerful, he would not allow evil and suffering to exist in his creation. But evil does exist. Therefore many people conclude that either God is not all-good (that's why he tolerates evil), or he is not all-powerful (and can't get rid of evil even though he wants to). The Bible gives a clear answer to this apparent contradiction.

The great Russian novelist Fyodor Dostoyevsky addresses the suffering of the innocent in all its poignancy in his novel *The Brothers*

Karamazov. In a challenge to his Christian brother, Ivan Karamazov tells the story of a young girl tormented, even tortured, by her parents. Ivan then asks: "Do you understand . . . why this infamy must be and is permitted?" Ivan insists that he cannot accept a God who allows the pointless suffering of a child. "Imagine that you are creating a fabric of human destiny with the object of making men happy in the end, giving them peace and rest at last, but that it was essential and inevitable to torture to death only one tiny creature—that baby beating its breast with its fist, for instance—and to found that edifice on its avenged tears, would you worship the architect on those conditions?"

The answer must be no. No sensitive person could say otherwise. But what's wrong here is the premise: the assumption that God would design a human destiny that required evil as a temporary stage in order to make people happy in the end. The God of Scripture does not need to build a temporary hell in order to produce heaven. He creates a world that is "very good" from the start (Gen. 1:31). God did not create evil. The absolute goodness of God is a first principle of Christian thinking.

Q 9: *If God didn't create evil, where did it come from?*

When things go horribly wrong, even die-hard atheists shake their fists at the God they say does not exist. We instinctively blame God for all our sorrows. Only the biblical answer tells us how God can be God—how he can be the ultimate reality and Creator of all things—and yet *not* be responsible for evil.

The Bible teaches that God is good and that he created a good universe. It also teaches that the universe today is marred by sin, death, and suffering. Since God is not the source of sin and suffering, there is only one possibility: that there is another source of sin, another being who can make moral choices and originate in God's world something that was not there before. This being need not be a second god, a second creator, for evil is not ultimate in the same way that good is.

Scripture teaches that evil came into God's creation through the free moral choices made by the first human beings, in response to the temptation of Satan, a fallen spirit. Like a plague, this evil spreads through all of history because of the free moral choices that humans continue to make.

In his goodness God allows finite humans to choose freely whether to submit to his good and wise authority. God's goodness is unaffected by humankind's rebellion, by its choice to do evil. Evil exists because of humankind's refusal to accept the good that God offers. God is not responsible for evil. We are.

This point must be burned into our understanding because in our utopian age so many people—even Christians—are prone to deny the reality of the Fall. I was recently talking to a young convert who said, "Aren't Adam and Eve just symbols for all humanity, and the Fall a symbol of the sin that traps all of us?" The answer is that the Fall cannot be reduced to a symbol without losing the distinctive Christian answer. The biblical understanding insists that the Fall is an event that actually happened at a particular point in time. God made the world good, and at some time, through an act of the will, humans rejected God's way and introduced evil—in truth, a rejection of the perfect Creator's way—into the creation.

> ## *[God] created the fact of freedom; we perform the acts of freedom. He made evil possible; man made evil actual.*
>
> Norman Geisler and Ron Brooks, *When Skeptics Ask*

If the Fall is merely a symbol for persistent sin, if sin has always been part of human nature and is intrinsic to it, then once again we are saying that God created evil. The poet Archibald MacLeish addresses the problem of evil in his poetic drama *J. B.*, which retells the story of Job in a modern setting. J. B. cannot accept a God who makes people imperfect and then punishes them for their imperfection. And he is right. The biblical answer to evil is not that God created human beings intrinsically flawed or sinful or incapable of choosing the good but rather that evil entered and marred that good creation.

It is important to emphasize the historical reality of Adam and Eve. Parts of Genesis may be poetic in their literary style, but the essential philosophical point in the story is that the universe God made was good and that a traumatic, ruinous, cataclysmic, disruptive change took place when sin entered as a result of humanity's choice to rebel against God's authority. Our choice threw creation out of joint. It distorted and disfigured the world, bringing in death and destruction.

That's why evil is so hateful, so repulsive. That's why we cry in the night against it. Our response is entirely appropriate. We sense that something is wrong, and we are right—something is.

God can comfort us in our sorrow and pain because he's on our side. He didn't create this distortion, and he hates it even more than we do. In the fight against evil, he is our Champion—*not* a cruel God inflicting evil on us.

Q 10: *Why did God allow us to disobey?*

God could have created us incapable of sin. He could have made sure that we were unable to make wrong moral choices. But then, of course, we would be less than human. We would be robots, like puppets on a stage, with God pulling every string. Free will is the basis of our human dignity. Because we are created in the image of God, we are capable of choosing to obey or not to obey. God has made us free and responsible moral agents.

The introduction of evil's possibility is the condition of our being free and responsible, both the gift and the price of human dignity.

Q 11: *Then why does a good God allow the consequences of evil to continue? Why doesn't he simply wipe out evil as soon as it appears on the scene?*

The only possible answer is that God *can't* wipe it out without violating his own nature. God's character is the standard of goodness and justice, and once evil and injustice exist, he must set it right again. God cannot ignore sin, overlook it, simply destroy the world, and start over. Once the scales of justice have been tipped, they must be balanced. Once the moral fabric of the universe has been torn, it must be mended. Otherwise we would not live in a moral universe. There is an objective, eternal, cosmic standard of justice, and its demands must be met. Evildoers must be punished; otherwise their free moral agency would have been a farce. For people to be fully human, their actions must have consequences and afford ultimate meaning in an eternal context.

In that case, your child might respond, the human race should have ended with Adam and Eve. They would have been punished for their rebellion, cast into the lake of fire, and that would have been the end of human history. Ah, but God is merciful as well as just, and he came up with a remarkable, astonishing, unthinkable alternative: He himself would bear the punishment for his creatures. God himself would enter the world of humanity and take on the suffering and death and judgment that his people had incurred. And that is exactly what he did: The Creator entered the creation and became a human being in order to bear the punishment for human sin.

This was not what anyone would expect. God faced the ugliness and brokenness of the world by becoming part of it. God in Christ grappled with violence and death by submitting to execution on a Roman cross. He met the demands of divine justice by submitting to judgment as a criminal and a sinner even though he had never sinned. So the Christian answer to suffering is not an idea, an argument, a philosophy. It's an event that *happened*. Just as evil entered human history through a definite act on the part of human beings, so salvation was accomplished through an act on the part of God.

The answer the Bible offers is not a passive principle but a Being who acts in history. Not an abstract logical concept but a divine Person. Not a new way of thinking but a new life. Jesus beat Satan at his own game. He took the worst that Satan could mete out and turned it into the means of salvation. "By his wounds we are healed," writes Isaiah (Isa. 53:5).

Evil has been defeated. At some time in the future there will be a world free of sin and suffering. The decisive battle has been won, a beachhead secured, the victory guaranteed. At the end of time there will be a new heaven and a new earth where "he will wipe every tear from their eyes" (Rev. 21:4).

This means that the suffering we endure today takes on a new meaning. It becomes our participation in establishing Christ's victory—both freedom from personal sin and justice in society. God uses the thorns and thistles that have infested the ground since the Fall to teach and chastise and transform us, making us ready for heaven and helping us to appreciate the magnitude of his goodness along the way. Suffering is transformed into a means of sanctification. As we turn to God in our sorrows, he enlarges our soul so that we rise above our pain, grow spiritually, gain new wisdom, and overcome evil with good.

An ancient document describing first-century martyrs of the church says that as they were being scourged, they "attained such towering strength of soul that not one of them uttered a cry or groan." That is how God uses suffering in the lives of all who turn to him: as a means of giving them "towering strength of soul."

Q 12: *Why would a good and loving God use suffering to change us and make us grow spiritually?*

A loving God uses whatever it takes—and for fallen beings it often takes pain. If you break a bone and the doctor has to reset it, it hurts. As fallen creatures we are metaphorically full of broken bones. And when God resets the broken bones of our character, it hurts.

Of course, at times we also bring suffering on ourselves. God allows us to experience the natural consequences of our own sin so that we may see how bad it really is and be drawn to repentance. At these times suffering operates like the pain in our finger when we touch a hot stove and say, "Ouch! I shouldn't have done that." Pain can have an instructive effect—what the writer of Hebrews had in mind when describing it as "chastisement" (Heb. 12:8, KJV). Sometimes we receive suffering as a loving Father's correction.

Not all suffering is a direct result of sin, however. Jesus makes that clear in the story of the blind man (see John 9). The disciples asked, Why was this man born blind? Because of his own sin or his parents' sin? And Jesus replied: "Neither. . . . This happened so that the work of God might be displayed in his life" (John 9:3). Jesus then proceeds to do the work of God by healing the man of his blindness. In other words, some of our disabilities are not our fault, but God chooses to work through them for his purposes as we turn to him for healing and wholeness.

The famous atheist Friedrich Nietzsche once uttered a profoundly biblical truth: "Men and women can endure any amount of suffering so long as they know the why to their existence." Much of the sting is taken out of the brokenness of the human condition if we can see it within some wider context of meaning and purpose. Only the Bible gives us that wider context—an eternal perspective. Evil is real, but it is not part of the original creation—it is not inherent in reality—and one day it will be cast out. Its hold on reality is only temporary. In the meantime, the wonder of God's character is that he can take even the worst of evils—the crucifixion of his sinless Son—and turn it to good ends: to defeat Satan; to save, strengthen, and purify us; and to bring glory and honor to himself. God's purposes are the context that give meaning and significance to suffering.

Augustine encapsulated the mystery of suffering in his famous doctrine of "Blessed Fault": "God judged it better to bring good out of evil than to suffer no evil at all." For God, enduring the pain involved in redeeming sinners was better than not creating human beings at all. Why is that? The question can be answered in a single word: Love. God loved us so much that even when he foresaw the sin and suffering that would darken his creation, he still chose to create us with a free will and human dignity. That is the profoundest mystery of all.

And the greatest news humanity has ever received is that there is a way out of the dilemma. Yes, we are fallen, and our fall has brought distortion to creation. But we don't need to be tormented by our guilt or the weight of sin. There is a way of redemption, through the atoning death and resurrection of Jesus Christ.

Q 13: *But aren't people really inherently good—or at least morally neutral?*

The terrifying truth is that we are not morally neutral. A friend of mine who is a renowned psychologist and an Orthodox Jew often makes the point that people, left to their own devices, with the assurance that they would never be caught or held accountable, will more often choose what is wrong than what is right. We are drawn toward evil; without powerful intervention we will choose it.

And yet many of our children are so steeped in education that is overly focused on the importance of self-esteem that they have little sense that they can do anything wrong—other than not loving themselves enough. They do not see themselves as sinners.

Not long ago MTV decided to tackle the subject of sin. A special news report, "The Seven Deadly Sins," featured interviews with pop celebrities and ordinary teens. They were asked to talk about the seven sins condemned by Christian tradition as the most dangerous: lust, pride, anger, envy, sloth, greed, and gluttony.

The program was intended to show that people still grapple with the same sins that have plagued human nature for millennia. But what it really showed is that modern young people are woefully ignorant of basic moral categories.

Take lust. Rap star Ice-T glared into the MTV camera and said, "Lust isn't a sin. . . . These are all dumb." One young man seemed to think sloth was a work break. "Sloth. . . . Sometimes it's good to sit back and give yourself personal time."

Actress Kirstie Alley snapped, "I don't think pride is a sin, and I think some idiot made that up. Who made these up anyway?"

When told that the seven deadly sins are a heritage of medieval theology, Alley showed a slight spark of contrition. She didn't mean "to knock monks or anything," she said. But really, the anti-ego thing didn't work for her.

That just about captures the tone of the whole program: No one seemed concerned about whether the seven deadly sins represent moral truth; the only standard was whether something enhances our self-esteem.

It's amazing that even in the context of talking about sin, there was not one word about moral responsibility, repentance, or objective standards of right and wrong.

MTV showed our moral confusion.

> ## As parents, we don't have to be fearful to admit we are sinners and need to come to Jesus and repent. We need to expose our children to the whole Christian doctrine, not just that God is love and wants to be your friend. We start there, but we go on to expose them to the doctrine of sin.
>
> Evelyn Christenson, *Parents and Teenagers*

And yet deep inside us we know the depths of our depravity. I think of the story of Yehiel Dinur, an Auschwitz survivor who testified at the war-crimes trial of Adolf Eichmann, one of the worst of the Holocaust masterminds. In the courtroom Dinur stared Eichmann in the eye and then suddenly broke into sobs. Was he overcome by hatred . . . by the horrifying memories . . . by the evil in Eichmann's face?

No. Dinur later explained that he realized that Eichmann was not the demonic personification of evil, as Dinur had expected, but an ordinary man. Dinur saw in Eichmann a reflection of himself: "I was afraid about myself," Dinur said. "I saw that I am capable to do this . . . exactly like he."

Dinur realized that "Eichmann is in all of us."

We are by nature evil and inclined to do evil. After listing a number of sins, Jesus said, "All these vile things come from within" (Mark 7:23, NLT).

This offends the modern mind because it directly challenges the dominant secular, utopian view that men and women are innately good and that their bad actions result from corrupt social influences.

Q 14: *Can't the world's problems be overcome with better education and social programs?*

This is what our children are learning in their public school classrooms and what they might understand by listening to the national news. Civilization will eradicate evil.

This notion first gained popularity two hundred years ago during the Enlightenment. Rousseau and other thinkers argued that through education people could eradicate sin and eventually build a perfect society.

This became one of the prevailing myths of our time. The sentiment permeated the Humanist Manifesto II: "By using technology wisely, we can control our environment, conquer poverty, . . . modify behavior, alter the course of human evolution and cultural development, . . . and provide humankind with unparalleled opportunity for achieving an abundant and meaningful life."

This is the humanist doctrine of sanctification by progress. Its seduction lies in its appeal to our pride: The obstacles are not in ourselves but in our stars—or in unemployment, racism, poverty, or mental illness. Alexander Solzhenitsyn called this myth "the benevolent concept according to which man—the master of the world—does not bear any evils within himself, and all the defects of life are caused by misguided social systems."

The record of gore and inhumanity of the twentieth century, from the ovens of the Holocaust to the killing fields of Cambodia to the nightly slaughter on America's streets, ought to jar us into sober reality. The truth is, the human race hasn't outgrown sin, nor can we. It lives within us. Jesus put it succinctly: "From within, out of a person's heart, come evil thoughts, sexual immorality, theft, murder, adultery, greed, wickedness, deceit. . . . All these vile things come from within; they are what defile you and make you unacceptable to God" (Mark

7:21-23, NLT).That message may seem out-of-date in light of all the high-tech wizardry and enlightened sophistry of this generation. But real progress, the kind that goes beyond satellites and fiber optics, comes from only one source: from the One who can cleanse the evil within us by creating clean hearts within us. He is our only real hope for progress, in this time or in any other.

People often resist this notion, though, and prefer to think other-wise—even when the truth is all around them.

> ### *Sin has always been an ugly word, but it has been made so in a new sense over the last half-century. It has been made not only ugly but passé. People are no longer sinful, they are only immature or underprivileged or frightened or, more particularly, sick.*
>
> Phyllis McGinley

A few years ago, while touring a Norwegian prison, I witnessed a tragic example of what happens when people ignore the reality of sin and try to "fix" it with a psychological program.

Norwegian officials brag that they employ the most humane and progressive methods of treatment anywhere in the world. The prison I visited was full of psychiatrists. So during my tour I asked the warden how many of the inmates, all of whom were serving time for severe crimes, were mental cases.

"Oh, all of them," she answered.

I frowned, puzzled. "What do you mean 'all of them'?" I asked.

"Well," she answered, "anyone who commits a crime this serious is obviously mentally unbalanced."

I realized that I was confronting firsthand a thoroughly Enlighten-ment mentality: There is no sin; people are basically good. So the only reason they might do something wrong is that they are mentally ill. The prison officials were determined to "cure" people through behavior modification and all of the other up-to-date psychological techniques.

But in the same prison I met a young woman who proved with her life that a worldview that denies the reality of sin is pure folly. She was a corrections officer and a Christian. "Oh, how they need to hear the gospel," she said as she thanked me for preaching. She was frustrated because she knew that unless criminals are confronted with their genuine moral culpability, their lives can never be transformed.

What happened a few days later confirmed in a horrible way the validity of her criticisms. She escorted a prison inmate out on a short furlough, and on the way home, he overpowered, raped, and murdered her.

To deny the reality of sin is not just unbiblical; it's also foolish. No amount of education or technology can overcome the evil that lies in our hearts (Prov. 14:12).

Q 15: *How could people like mass murderer Jeffrey Dahmer do the things they do unless they're sick?*

Have you met the Jeffrey Dahmers of the world? I have.

In 1981 I visited death row at the maximum security prison in Menard, Illinois, and one of the prisoners asked to speak with me alone. He was a middle-aged man with neatly brushed, silver-streaked hair, a warm smile, and intelligent eyes. Except for his shackles and chains, he could have been a genial high school principal or a friendly pharmacist.

But that man was John Wayne Gacy Jr., who had sexually abused and murdered thirty-three young men. As we sat in a small interview room and talked, Gacy spoke quite rationally. And as I thought of his crimes, I kept telling myself that he had to be sick.

He *was* sick, but he was sick with sin that had erupted into horrific evil. Only as I reminded myself that he was sick with the same sin that dwells in all of us was I able to spend one hour facing him across a table—and then to pray with him.

Jeffrey Dahmer's trial revolved around the issue of his sanity. No one disputed that Dahmer had committed unspeakably grisly crimes. Everyone asked the question we're addressing here: How could a sane person have done those things?

Yet a Milwaukee jury, confronted with ghastly murder, cannibalism, and necrophilia, concluded that Dahmer was not insane—just evil.

There is a tendency today to try to find excuses for all sorts of evil behavior. Novelist Saul Bellow calls this the "golden age of exoneration." In criminal trials the defense is often based on the fact that the accused came from a dysfunctional home or that he or she had some other environmental disadvantage.

This kind of defense has grown so common that it even has its own name—the "Twinkie defense," named for the famous 1978 case in which a man pleaded temporary insanity after shooting the mayor and the city supervisor in San Francisco. His argument was that he had eaten a steady diet of junk food that raised his blood sugar and caused him to act irrationally.

We look for excuses because we're unwilling to face the reality of the human condition. To be sure, some people are mentally unbalanced, but these are exceptions. I've been in six hundred prisons around the world in the last twenty-five years, and I can tell you that the cause of crime is not mental sickness. It is sin. People make wrong moral choices and must be held accountable. When we don't get this right, we create travesties like the episode in the Norwegian prison.

Q 16: *Is there a hell?*

I've been asked a similar question before, in a surprising context. During a visit to England I gave an address at a meeting attended by the eminent historian Paul Johnson, author of *Modern Times*. At the end of my talk Johnson looked at me and said, "I think the biggest problem facing the modern age is what to do about the doctrine of hell. What do you think?"

I was taken aback; the question had nothing to do with my talk. But as Johnson expanded on his question, I realized how right he was.

When the Christian church does not clearly teach the doctrine of hell, society loses an important anchor. In a sense, the concept of hell gives meaning to our lives. It tells us that the moral choices we make day by day have eternal significance, that our behavior has consequences lasting to eternity, that God himself takes our choices seriously.

When people don't believe in a final judgment, they don't feel ultimately accountable for their actions. There is no firm leash holding back sinful impulses. There is no fear of God in their hearts, and as the book of Judges puts it, everyone does what is right in his or her own eyes (Judg. 21:25).

The doctrine of hell is not just some dusty theological holdover from the Middle Ages. It has significant social consequences. Without a conviction of ultimate justice, people's sense of moral obligation dissolves, and social bonds are broken.

Of course, these considerations are not the most important reason to believe in hell. Jesus repeatedly issued warnings that if we turn away from God in this life, we will be alienated from God eternally.

And yet, although "the wages of sin is death," Paul also says that "the gift of God is eternal life in Christ Jesus our Lord" (Rom. 6:23). While breath remains, it is never too late to turn to God in repentance, and when we ask for forgiveness, God eagerly grants it. (For further discussion, see question 41: "What happens to people who die without ever hearing about Christ?")

Q 17: *Are there really such beings as angels and devils?*

The Bible is full of accounts of messengers from God helping, protecting, confronting, and ministering to people. Angels appear to Abraham and Sarah. Jacob wrestles with an angel. Angelic beings minister to the prophet Elijah. And in the most famous angelic appearance of all, an angel announces the advent of Jesus to his mother, Mary. In biblical accounts angels aren't cute, pudgy babies with wings. The first thing an angel says is, "Don't be afraid." In other words, real angels are a fearsome sight. They are mighty warriors in the great cosmic battle between good and evil.

These days, however, many claims about angelic activity are counterfeit. The angels of New Age thinkers don't sound very much like the ones in Scripture. The Bible calls real angels ministering spirits, but they are definitely not our personal servants.

New Agers tell of angels that appear on command, like genies, to change a tire on a deserted road or to make a bus slow down and pick someone up. These angels never ever confront or challenge anyone. They make no demands on our behavior or character. These are the "imaginary guides" of the New Age movement, not real angels.

Devils are fallen angels—angels in rebellion against God. And they are as real as their heavenly counterparts, although Christians should be wary of attributing every evil event to their influence.

Often people actually distract themselves from the real issues of the Christian life by ascribing too much influence both to angels and devils. It's an illusion to think that the kingdom of God exerts its influence in this world primarily by means of angelic beings. That's *our* job. We are the body of Christ, and it's up to us to make his presence real to our neighbors. Similarly, the Scriptures teach us that *we* are responsible for most of the world's evil. We cannot avoid our responsibility for evil—or even exempt our neighbors from responsibility for their actions—by seeing all of life simply as "spiritual warfare" in which humanity serves merely as so many pawns of supernatural powers. The devil and his followers are quite real, but again, pure human choice accounts for most of the world's evil.

KEY POINTS IN BRIEF

✓ God did not create evil. The absolute goodness of God is a first principle of Christian thinking.

✓ Evil came into the world through the first human beings' own choice to rebel against God. Evil spreads like a plague through history because of the free moral choices that humans continue to make.

✓ Free will is the basis of human dignity.

✓ God allows the consequences of evil to continue in order to redeem them and to demonstrate and maintain his character as a good God.

✓ God himself entered the world in Christ in order to bear the punishment for human sin and reestablish the communion of God and humanity.

✓ The suffering we endure today becomes our participation in establishing Christ's victory.

✓ Not all suffering is a direct result of sin. But God can use any evil to bring about healing and wholeness.

✓ Because God loves us so much, it was better for him to endure the pain involved in redeeming evil than not to create human beings at all. This is a profound mystery.

✓ We are not morally neutral or innately good but are inclined to evil.

✓ To deny the reality of sin is foolish and creates disastrous unintended effects.

✓ Jesus repeatedly issued warnings that if we turn away from God in this life, we will be alienated from God eternally. The reality of hell is a sign of how much God respects our choices.

CHAPTER 3

Does Modern Science Disprove
the Bible and Christianity?
Science, Evolution, and Intelligent Design

Q 18: *Is the universe all there is?*

Our teenagers may ask questions such as, Is what we see all there is? or Our scientific understanding of the cosmos doesn't leave any place for God, does it? These questions open up one of the most important topics of our time: evolution.

First, let's address the broad topic and then explore related questions that are often answered in ways that undermine Christianity.

Many scientists do believe that the universe is self-existent—that God is not necessary—and that life is the result of chance occurrences. They believe this not for scientific reasons but for philosophical ones. They are committed to a philosophy called *naturalism.* Naturalism seeks to understand the world and life itself through natural cause and effect alone. In fact, naturalism argues that only things that can be empirically verified—known with the five senses—are real. God, goodness, beauty, even human consciousness itself (as more than a series of electrochemical reactions) simply go out the window.

The bonus for scientists is that they decide on what's real and what's unreal because they believe that they are the only ones who have the right method to investigate reality. Their presumption on this matter becomes clear in the debate over whether creation and evolution can be taught side by side in science classrooms as competing theories. The scientists who are dogmatic naturalists will have none of this. They say they know what's real: Naturalistic science is real; religion is simply wishful thinking.

But these judgments are not scientific; they are philosophical, even religious. They are also wrong. To argue against naturalism, we first have to point out its prejudices and presumptions.

Next time you're in a bookstore, browse through the science section for some startling titles: *The Mind of God, Theories of Everything,* and *Dreams of a Final Theory.* These books promise that physics is on the brink of finding a supertheory capable of explaining everything in the universe. In other words, many scientists are urging us to find ultimate truth not in religion but in physics.

Consider Stephen Hawking's runaway best-seller *A Brief History of Time.* Hawking promises that science will eventually give us "a complete understanding of . . . existence." A big step toward that goal is finding a unified theory of the four fundamental forces of nature: the electromagnetic force, the weak nuclear force, the strong nuclear force, and gravity.

Many physicists believe that the four fundamental forces were unified in the earliest moments of the big bang, when the universe began. If you assume that the universe is a closed system of natural causes and effects, then those initial conditions determined everything else that has ever happened in the history of the cosmos. A theory explaining those initial conditions would thus be the key to explaining the entire cosmos by purely natural causes. Then physics could finally dispense with *super*natural causes—such as a divine Creator.

In Hawking's words, a unified theory "would be the ultimate triumph of human reason—for then we would know the mind of God." Hawking doesn't believe in God. What he really means is that humans would then attain godlike omniscience; we would prove to ourselves that we are qualified to replace God.

(Does this sound familiar—reminiscent of Adam and Eve's Eden temptation: the serpent's promise that eating of the tree of the knowledge of good and evil would make them equal to God in knowledge? This temptation is still a powerful force.)

Supplanting God is often the motivation in the search for a unified theory. In *Reason in the Balance,* Berkeley professor Phillip Johnson says that such a theory would be so highly theoretical that it would be impossible to confirm by experiment. Which means it would, strictly speaking, not be scientific at all; its appeal would be philosophical or religious.

> *Naturalism is a metaphysical doctrine, which means simply that it states a particular view of what is ultimately real and unreal.*
>
> Phillip Johnson, *Reason in the Balance*

The question at the core of science today is whether God exists or whether nature is all there is. British physicist Paul Davies puts it bluntly in his book *The Mind of God.* There, Davies says that Hawking's theories could well "be quite wrong." But so what? The real issue, Davies explains, "is whether or not some sort of supernatural act is necessary to start the universe off. If a plausible scientific theory can be constructed that will explain the origin of the entire physical universe, then at least we know a scientific explanation is possible, whether or not the current theory is right."

Did you understand what he's saying? Davies is admitting that for him *it doesn't matter* whether a scientific theory is right or wrong; it matters only whether the theory gets rid of the supernatural. This amounts to admitting that even a myth is acceptable, as long as it's a *naturalistic* myth—as long as it reassures scientists they don't have to worry about a divine Creator.

When your children start asking about the origins of the universe, start answering their questions by pointing out that many basic "scientific" judgments are not scientific (they cannot be proven). They are philosophical judgments, even religious ones. The idea of a self-existent universe is a prime example. This is not a conclusion of science. It's a presupposition—a starting point—of the atheistic philosophy of naturalism.

Q 19: *But haven't scientists proven experimentally that life came about by chance?*

I'm afraid this is the impression many young people are given in their science classes.   ,

Back in the 1960s, for example, we read headlines claiming that scientists were about to conjure up life in a test tube. Biochemists discovered they could mix chemicals—ammonia, methane, and water—zap them with an electric spark, and create amino acids, the building blocks of proteins.

The scientific community was euphoric. But then things ground to a halt. The amino acids never did form proteins or evolve into a living cell. And critics charged that even the amino acids were obtained only by rigging the experiment, essentially by cheating.

You see, origin-of-life experiments are supposed to be reenactments of what could have happened in a warm pond on our planet in its early stages. The most realistic experiment would be pouring various chemicals into water and mixing them up. But no researcher ever does that because it doesn't yield anything. Instead, scientists tinker with the experiment at several points.

For example, in a real pond, there would be all sorts of chemical reactions and environmental variables, many of them canceling out the reactions scientists need. They must resort to intervention: purifying the ingredients, screening out light waves harmful to amino acids, and immediately removing linked amino acids to prevent disintegration. The upshot is that even the most successful experiments tell us nothing about what can happen in nature. They tell us only what can happen when brilliant scientists direct and manipulate conditions.

So experiments don't prove life can arise spontaneously in nature. On the contrary, they give experimental evidence that life can be created only by an intelligent agent directing and controlling the process.

Despite the fact that scientists haven't been able to activate amino acids into any evolving forms, the idea that life evolved from a primordial soup has been elaborated into a network of complex theories.

But at the 1993 International Conference on the Origin of Life, the practicing chemists turned thumbs down on all the popular theories. What has chemists stymied is how to concentrate all the right ingredients in one place. Chemicals link up only when energy, heat, or electricity is applied. This means most origin-of-life theories start with a chemical soup heated by volcanoes or zapped by lightning. But there's a fly in this chemical soup.

The chemical reactions that should form DNA are reversible. The molecules that come together can separate again. It's easier to break the links than to make them. What does that mean for origin-of-life theories? If you simulate the origin of life in a test tube, any organic compounds that form will quickly break up again. You never get enough of them concentrated in one place to form DNA. This one fact makes it impossible for life to have evolved on the early Earth.

By the same token, a chemical soup will never form DNA. For life to emerge, the right organic compounds need to be sorted out and protected so they don't break up. But nature doesn't come equipped with any sorting mechanisms. There's only one thing that can select and sort: an intelligent agent.

Furthermore, not a single one of these theories addresses a crucial piece of the puzzle—what scientists call the "sequence problem": If life evolved from a soup of chemicals, how did the components line up in the right sequence?

For example, many origin-of-life theories start with protein. A protein consists of a chain of amino acids. As we've said, scientists have discovered that you can mix amino acids in a flask and zap them with an electric spark, and they will link up into short chains. But the dirty little secret of these experiments is that the amino acid chains don't resemble living proteins in the slightest. The sequence is all wrong. *The Soul of Science* quotes Dean Kenyon: "One thing that stands out is that you do not get ordered sequences of amino acids. . . . If we thought we were going to see a lot of spontaneous ordering, something must have been wrong with our theory." And in *The Creation Hypothesis* scientist Klaus Dose makes a similar point. The primordial soup experiment, he says, has "led to a better perception of the immensity of the problem of the origin of life on earth rather than to its solution."

To understand the "immensity of the problem," imagine that amino acids are Scrabble letters and that you want to spell the word *protein*. Of course, you or I could arrange Scrabble letters in the right sequence easily. But we do it by using something beyond natural forces. We use intelligence. The missing ingredient in standard theories of life's origin is an intelligent agent. The random results scientists obtain have never overcome the sequence problem—the amino acids just don't know how to spell. The test tube experiments of scientists have only proven how much intelligent design goes into approximating God's creation of life.

(If these paragraphs have made you curious to dig deeper, you will find more thorough explanations of these ideas in part 2 of *How Now Shall We Live?*)

Q 20: *Even if scientists haven't specifically proven how life came about, don't they have evidence that evolution is a fact, not just a theory?*

The evidence for evolution often comes down to how scientists define the word *evolution*. The meaning of the word is vitally important, and yet it has a way of changing without notice. The first thing we must learn to do is to distinguish *microevolution* from *macroevolution*.

Microevolution is cyclical variation within the type. For example, on the Galapagos Islands in the Pacific, finches exhibit shifts in the size and shape of their beaks in response to environmental conditions. Over several generations the beaks of finches have changed shape, and that shape depends on whether longer or shorter beaks are better for food gathering. Similarly, in England some species of birds have learned how to pick the foil cap from bottles of fresh milk left at the door. They adapt to the food resources of their environment. These and thousands of other cases of adaptation are largely not controversial. But is this evolution?

This is where the problem arises. If variation in finches' beaks or birds' ability to steal caps from bottles is what biologists mean by evolution, then call me an evolutionist. But of course that's not the only meaning.

There's another meaning for the term, one that's much more controversial.

Macroevolution is a process that supposedly creates innovations such as new complex organs or new body parts. Darwinists typically "claim that macro evolution is just micro evolution continued over a very long time through a mechanism called natural selection," writes Phillip Johnson in his book *Defeating Darwinism*. The claim is highly controversial because the "mechanism of macro evolution has to be able to design and build very complex structures like wings and eyes and brains," and "it has to have done this reliably again and again."

The trouble is that plenty of experiments have shown that small changes do not accumulate to make large changes. If scientists stick to actual observations, all they have ever seen is the modification of existing categories of living things, not the rise of new categories.

Macroevolution also assumes that change in the living world is unlimited. The trouble is that the only changes actually observed are limited. Farmers can breed for sweeter corn, bigger roses, or faster horses, but they still end up with corn, roses, and horses. No one has ever produced a new kind of organism.

Evolutionists take these small-scale changes and, once again, extrapolate them. They speculate what might happen if minor changes are added up and are extended back millions of years into the misty past.

There's nothing wrong with extrapolation per se, but this particular one is unsound. The variation induced by breeding does not continue at a steady rate through each generation. Instead, it is rapid at first and then levels off. Eventually it reaches a ceiling that breeders cannot cross. If they try, the organism grows weaker and more prone to disease until it finally becomes sterile and dies out. So breeders can breed for bigger roses, but they'll never get one as big as a sunflower.

Darwin believed nature could select among organisms the way a breeder does, which is why he called his theory *natural selection.* He proposed that life evolved gradually, by imperceptibly tiny steps, from the simplest one-celled organism to the most complex birds and beasts.

> *Fossil evidence should on the whole support the claim that today's complex organisms evolved step-by-gradual-step from specific common ancestors. . . . It is generally conceded today, however, that fossil species are remarkably stable over long periods of time and the appearance of new forms is typically abrupt.*
>
> Phillip Johnson, *Reason in the Balance*

But this continuous chain is nowhere to be seen. In the world today, bears and beavers and bats are all quite distinct. There are clear gaps between major biological categories, with no blurring of the boundaries.

In answer to this, Darwin suggested that the missing links have died out and would one day be found in the fossil record. In response to Darwin's suggestion, the history of paleontology is largely a history of the search for the missing links.

If Darwin were right, the fossil record should show literally millions of transitional forms. But that's precisely what it does *not* show. Yes, the fossils do show that life was often very different from what it is today. Some forms of elephants were once hairy: the woolly mammoths. Some forms of reptiles were once gigantic: the *Tyrannosaurus rex.* But here's the important point: Those strange forms still fit clearly within the same basic categories known today. Elephants were still elephants; reptiles were still reptiles. The same gaps that exist in the fossil record still exist in the living world today.

In other words, based on actual observations, the bottom line is this: All that scientists have ever seen is the modification of existing categories of living things, not the rise of new categories.

What the naturalistic evolutionists have been able to prove doesn't approach the theory's claims.

Q 21: *Isn't it possible that evolution and creation are both true?*

There's a name for this line of reasoning: theistic evolution. The idea that perhaps evolution was directed by God appears to be an attractive solution and one frequently embraced by Christian students trying to reconcile their faith with the teachings of their science teachers.

Evolution's basic premise makes this approach inherently flawed, however. Imagining that evolutionary theory allows for a Creator—that evolution could be a God-guided process—is exactly what establishment scientists do not allow.

Prominent Darwinists from Stephen Gould to Richard Dawkins to John Maynard Smith insist that evolution is unguided and purposeless. As Phillip Johnson puts it in *Defeating Darwinism,* "The Darwinian theory doesn't just say that God created slowly [over millions of years]. It says that naturalistic evolution is the creator—and God had nothing to do with it."

Evolution in the Darwinian sense is both mindless and godless. As the famous evolutionist George Gaylord Simpson put it, "Man is the result of a purposeless and natural process that did not have him in mind."

Darwinists cannot afford to abandon this claim, Johnson says, because their whole approach is founded on naturalism, the doctrine that nature is all there is. Darwinian evolution tries to explain how nature did this without any assistance from a supernatural entity. Thus, an attempt to reconcile Darwinian evolution theories with creation "is an evasion of the conflict, not a resolution to it," Johnson warns.

People are kidding themselves when they think they can believe in both creation and evolution. What's at stake is not merely the details of evolution versus the details of Genesis in the Bible. Rather, the issue is the stark, fundamental claim that life is the product of impersonal forces versus the claim that it is the creation of an intelligent Designer.

Q 22: How can we distinguish things that "just happen" from those that are created?

This question about distinguishing natural phenomena from those produced by intelligent design gets to the heart of the creation-evolution debate.

Imagine we are touring Egypt and suddenly see huge pyramidal structures rising out of the sand. Immediately we recognize the work of an intelligent agent. No one would mistake the pyramids of Egypt for a natural phenomenon. This ability to distinguish human workmanship from the products of nature is crucial in archaeology. Digging through the dust in Mesopotamia, archaeologists have to decide whether they have found a chunk of rock or a chunk of broken pottery.

Imagine we're walking along the beach and come across a small square box booming out a rock song like Kurt Cobain's "Smells Like Teen Spirit." Immediately we recognize a different level of order from the surrounding noise of the surf. We recognize what scientists call *complexity*.

Or imagine we're looking up at the sky and see something that looks rounded and white like a cloud, but across the middle of this object is printed the word *Goodyear*. Without a doubt we conclude that this is no cloud, and we may even wave to the people riding in the blimp.

It's true that the physical world can produce a regular pattern, such as the sound of the surf pounding on the beach. But nature cannot produce complexity. You see, common everyday experience gives us a good idea of the things nature is capable of creating by itself—and the things that can be created only by an intelligent source.

Based on common experience—and after all, science is supposed to be based on experience—it's a logical argument that life was created and designed by an intelligent Agent. Which is exactly what Christians have always believed.

We are not inferring design from what we do not know, but from what we do know.

Michael Behe, *Darwin's Black Box*

Q 23: *Aren't you just giving God credit for what you don't understand?*

Does any of the scientific evidence support the view that God had to be involved? To answer this question, let's delve deeper into the issue of creation and design. At the core of life is the DNA molecule. Geneticists tell us the structure of DNA is identical to a language. It acts like a code, a molecular communication system within the cell. In other words, when geneticists probed the nucleus of the cell, they came across something analogous to *Goodyear* written in the sky or "Smells Like Teen Spirit" heard on the beach.

Of course, DNA contains a lot more information than these simple phrases. The average DNA molecule contains as much information as a city library! Think about that. So if *Goodyear* had to be written by an intelligent being, how much more the DNA code.

Some of the newer discoveries about DNA offer even more powerful evidence for God's role in creation. Since the 1960s, scientists have known that the DNA molecule is like a written message containing instructions for every living structure, from fish to flowers. But in higher organisms, the DNA code is broken up by sections of what looks like sheer nonsense—long DNA sequences that don't seem to mean anything. Scientists have dubbed these sequences "junk" DNA.

Kenneth Miller, a biologist at Brown University, uses junk DNA to criticize the idea of divine creation. How can we believe God directly created us, Miller argues, if the human genome is littered with genetic trash? An intelligent Creator wouldn't write nonsense into our genes.

But one researcher's junk can be another's jewels. Other scientists have discovered that junk DNA does important work after all. It functions to correct errors and regulate genes, turning them on and off at appropriate times. In short, what once appeared to be nonsense DNA actually makes very good sense.

It seems that the foes of the creation view spoke too soon—and put their feet squarely in their mouths. DNA actually provides remarkable evidence for creation, giving a new twist to the classic design argument presented nearly two hundred years ago by the English clergyman William Paley. He talked in terms of finding a watch on a beach. Anyone finding such a complex gadget would assume that an intelligent being designed it.

Today science offers a much more striking analogy than any that William Paley could give—namely, the identical structure in written messages and the DNA molecule. Suddenly the design argument has become much more compelling.

Nevertheless, schools continue to teach evolution to students. The National Association of Biology Teachers has recently released a position statement on the teaching of evolution, a statement that stomps all over even the possibility of a Creator. "The diversity of life on earth," the biologists grandly announced, "is the outcome of evolution: an unsupervised, impersonal . . . process," governed by "natural selection, chance . . . and changing environments."

Creation beliefs, they added sternly, "have no place in the science classroom."

No wonder our kids are confused. These teachers are behaving as if the debate between Darwinism and creationism is all over and the Darwinists won, when the evidence supporting Darwinism is actually getting weaker and weaker.

The problem is, the case for creationism isn't easy to explain either.

Perhaps William Steig's recently released children's story *Yellow and Pink* best illustrates the case for creation. The story opens with a pair of wooden puppets, one painted pink, the other yellow, lying on a scrap of newspaper. Suddenly the yellow puppet sits up.

"Who are we?" he asks. "How [did we get] to be here?"

"Someone must have made us," replies the pink puppet.

The yellow puppet can't accept that. "I say we're an accident," he declares. "Somehow or other we just happened."

The pink puppet begins to laugh. "You mean these arms I can move this way and that . . . this breathing nose, these walking feet, all of this just happened by some kind of fluke? That's preposterous!"

"Don't laugh," the yellow puppet says. "With enough time . . . lots of unusual things could happen. . . . Suppose a branch broke off a tree and fell on a sharp rock . . . so that one end split open and made legs."

And then, he goes on eagerly, "This piece of wood froze and the ice split the mouth open. [And our] eyes . . . could have been made by . . . woodpeckers."

The pink puppet isn't convinced. "Explain this," he says. "How come we're painted the way we are? . . . How come we can see out of these holes the woodpecker made? And hear?"

Just then, a man comes along and scoops up the puppets. On the last page of the book, we see the yellow puppet—the one who was convinced that life "just happened"—whisper a question to his pink friend. "Who is this guy?"

Like the puppets, biologists speculate about life's origins. And, just like the yellow puppet, they sometimes come up with bizarre solutions that exclude even the possibility of a Creator. William Steig's amusing story shows how implausible the "impersonal, unsupervised" theory really is. When biologists reject God, they have to come up with some other explanation, however improbable, for how life began.

But perhaps best of all, the story beautifully illustrates how asking these hard questions and pondering the necessity of a Creator may ultimately lead your teenager to wonder, like the yellow puppet, "Who is this guy?"

Q 24: *Besides DNA coding, are there any other positive arguments for creation?*

Yes. In fact, there's a whole group of scientists who are now pursuing the implications of intelligent design for science.

As evidence for intelligent design, this group points especially to the *anthropic principle* and *irreducible complexity.*

The anthropic principle states that the physical structure of the universe is exactly what it must be in order to support life. For a familiar example, take water. Unlike most other substances, when water freezes, it expands and floats. If water didn't have this unique property, then in cold weather, lakes and rivers would freeze all the way down to the bottom, and all fish would die.

Or think about the position of our planet. If Earth were only slightly closer to the sun, it would be too hot to support life. But if Earth were farther away from the sun, it would be too cold to support life.

Isn't it a marvelous "coincidence" that our planet is just where it is in the solar system?

Another cosmic "coincidence" is the strength of gravity. Assuming that the universe began with a big bang, if the force of gravity had been just slightly stronger, that extra tug would long ago have pulled the cosmos together and caused it to collapse in on itself. On the other hand, if the force of gravity had been just the tiniest bit weaker, then it wouldn't have been strong enough to condense the original gas cloud into stars and galaxies.

The fact that gravity is just the force needed to create the universe is, in the words of one scientist, "a gigantic fluke—or divine intervention."

It's the same with electrical force. Every tree, every blade of grass is made of atoms, which contain electrons and protons. The electron has an electrical charge that balances exactly the charge of the proton.

What would happen if they weren't precisely balanced? If, say, the electron carried more charge than the proton, every atom in the universe would be negatively charged. Since like charges repel, the atoms would repel each other, and the universe would explode apart.

The anthropic principle makes a chance creation so improbable as to be absurd.

Scientist Michael Behe has proposed what he calls the theory of irreducible complexity. In his 1993 book *Darwin's Black Box,* Behe disputes

Darwin's theory that small changes over time can result in whole new species. He points out that the small changes that appear in species as a result of genetic mutation are not advantageous. More important, many structures within the body, the eye for example, are "irreducibly complex"; eyes work only as the result of coordination among many and varied parts that all have to be coordinated toward one end—sight. The retina's rods and cones are useless without the lenses of the outer eye, which would be purposeless except for the optic nerve, etc.

Behe uses a homey example of irreducible complexity: the mouse-trap. A mousetrap cannot be assembled gradually, he points out. You cannot start with a wooden platform and catch a few mice, add a spring and catch a few more mice, add a hammer, and so on. No, to even *start* catching mice, all the parts of the trap must be assembled from the outset. The mousetrap doesn't work until all its parts are present and working together.

> *If it could be demonstrated that any complex organ existed which could not possibly have been formed by numerous, successive, slight modifications, my theory would absolutely break down.*
>
> Charles Darwin, *The Origin of Species*

Behe conducted much of his work within the context of the individual cell, which was once thought to be a relatively crude or simple structure but now is understood to be vastly complex. Many structures within the living cell are like the mousetrap; they involve an entire system of interacting parts all working together. If one part were to evolve in isolation, the entire system of interacting parts would stop functioning; and since, according to Darwinism, natural selection preserves the forms that function better than their rivals, the nonfunctioning system would be eliminated by natural selection.

Therefore, there is no possible Darwinian explanation of how irreducibly complex structures and systems came into existence.

"The simplicity that was once expected to be the foundation of life," Behe says, "has proven to be a phantom; instead, systems of horrendous, irreducible complexity inhabit the cell. The resulting realization that life was designed by an intelligence is a shock to us in the 20th century who have gotten used to thinking of life as the result of simple natural laws."

Many scientists such as Behe are pursuing the implications of intelligent design, and they believe that their presupposition—that the universe was indeed brought into being by an intelligent agent—may well open up important avenues of inquiry that other scientists, blinded by naturalism, have been unable to pursue.

Q 25: *If science really hasn't proven evolution, why is it still accepted and taught in school as fact?*

People who don't believe in evolution are viewed as "uneducated." And that includes our teenagers. You need to be aware of the extreme pressure your teenagers are under to accept evolution as a fact. Going against the evolutionist tide at school can have severe consequences. It's really tough for kids to resist the appeal of "what everyone knows"—the secular position.

For example, Danny Phillips was a bright, motivated high school student who wrote a paper criticizing a classroom video that presented evolutionary theory as fact. His criticism was intelligently argued and persuasive, and school authorities agreed to stop using the video.

Immediately, however, the press pounced on the boy. A prominent evolutionist attacked him as an "enemy of learning." Letters poured in to the *Denver Post* calling Danny and his supporters "religious fanatics," "scientific illiterates," and "know-nothings."

Unfortunately, criticizing Darwinian evolution in school triggers a common American myth that those who believe in creation must be ignorant fundamentalist reactionaries. The origin of that myth is a 1960 film called *Inherit the Wind*, based on a play of the same name.

Many people think the film is a lightly fictionalized account of the 1925 Scopes "monkey trial," in which the brilliant defense attorney Clarence Darrow squared off with an ill-prepared and disastrously overconfident William Jennings Bryan for the prosecution. But in reality the film is a masterful work of propaganda.

Inherit the Wind tells the story of Bert Cates, a dedicated high school teacher who teaches his class about evolution, thus violating a state law. Cates is arrested, and the subsequent trial turns into a media circus.

Cates's attorney, Henry Drummond, makes a fool of prosecutor Matthew Harrison Brady, who is portrayed as a fundamentalist Christian. The townspeople are cast in the role of ignorant, hate-filled bigots.

A whole generation of Americans has grown up with these images. Schoolchildren read the play, and the film is shown in classrooms around the country. Never mind that it's a complete distortion of what happened in the real Scopes trial.

In reality the trial was staged by the American Civil Liberties Union. Scopes was never arrested, and Dayton (Tennessee) residents, far from being wild-eyed bigots, demonstrated the best of southern hospitality to the outside observers and reporters who flocked to their town. An excellent book that sets the record straight is Ed Larson's *Summer for the Gods.*

Yet it's the play and the movie, not the real events, that have shaped the common stereotypes.

The pervasive myth equating creation beliefs with ignorance has led most schools to teach science in absolute terms of what "really exists," that nature is ultimately all there is.

Q 26: *Why might admitting the existence of a Creator threaten educators?*

Our previously cited authority Phillip Johnson is a pugnacious law professor who travels to campuses challenging Darwinian evolution. In his book *Reason in the Balance* he says: "I have found that any discussion with modernists about the weaknesses of the theory of evolution quickly turns into a discussion of politics, particularly sexual politics." Why? Because liberals "typically fear that any discrediting of naturalistic evolution will end in women being sent to the kitchen, gays to the closet, and abortionists to jail."

For better or worse, we have inherited a view of science as methodologically atheistic.

Nancy Murphy, *Perspective on Science and Christian Faith*

In other words, in the debate over creation and evolution, people instinctively sense that much more is at stake than a scientific theory. What is accepted as scientific truth inescapably shapes one's views on a host of moral issues. People sense that acknowledging the existence of a Creator God calls for a response.

If nature is all there is, then there is no God, and ethical ideals and standards are not based on what God says; instead, they're based on what human beings think.

If God exists and he created us for a purpose, then we are obliged to live in conformity to God's created order—the laws of nature and God's moral law.

Q 27: *Are you sure Christianity isn't against science?*

I certainly am sure, but many contemporary advocates of science admittedly want to give the impression that Christianity is opposed to science.

Very soon, "the practice of religion must be regarded as antiscience," wrote John Maddox, editor of *Nature,* the world's most prestigious science journal.

That would be a big surprise to the people who *founded* modern science. Most of the early scientists—Copernicus, Newton, Linnaeus—were Christians. In fact, historians tell us that Christianity actually helped inspire the scientific revolution.

Consider a few examples. In pagan cultures, the world seemed alive with river goddesses, sun gods, astral deities. But Genesis 1 stands in stark contrast to all that. Nature is not divine; it is God's handiwork. The sun and moon are not gods; they are merely lights placed in the sky to serve God's purposes.

The pagan teaching proved to be a roadblock for science: As long as nature commanded religious worship, digging too closely into her secrets was deemed irreverent. But Christians believed that nature was not to be feared and worshiped. In this context—and only in this context—could nature become an object of scientific study.

Another crucial assumption for science is that nature is orderly. This assumption also was a result of Christian beliefs. The belief that God is rational and trustworthy implies that his creation is rational and ordered. The early scientists described that order as *natural law*. Today this phrase is so common we may not realize how unique it once was. Yet as historian A. R. Hall points out, no other culture used the word *law* in relation to nature. The idea of laws in nature came from the biblical teaching that God is both Creator and Lawgiver.

> ## *This most beautiful system of sun, planets, and comets could only proceed from the counsel and dominion of an intelligent and powerful Being.*
>
> Isaac Newton, quoted in *The Soul of Science*

Even the experimental method of science has roots in Christianity. Since it is *God's* rationality that orders nature and not our own, we cannot sit in an ivory tower and do science by sheer rational deduction. Instead, we must do experiments and see what happens.

For example, when Galileo wanted to find out whether a ten-pound weight falls to the ground more quickly than a one-pound weight, he didn't argue about the "nature" of weight, as was typical among philosophers of his day. Instead, he dropped cannonballs off the Leaning Tower of Pisa and watched what happened.

Some historians believe the story of Galileo is apocryphal, but the point still stands: Galileo and other early scientists explicitly argued in their writings that God's ways are not necessarily our ways—that God's ways in nature have to be discovered by experimentation and observation.

Q 28: *Didn't the Catholic Church's persecution of Galileo prove its opposition to science?*

The story of Galileo has always provided rich fodder for critics of religion. They love to cite it as the textbook case of Christian hostility to science.

In 1995 even the Roman Catholic Church seemed to concur. Galileo was right after all, blared the headlines. News reports announced that the Roman Catholic Church officially revoked its condemnation of Galileo, imposed more than three centuries ago. Pope John Paul II admitted that the church made a tragic mistake in forcing Galileo to recant his conviction that Earth goes around the sun.

But the real story is not a simple tale of good guys versus bad guys. The pope who condemned Galileo was not opposed to his *scientific* ideas. In fact, the pope was once a member of a group of Galileo's supporters. What actually concerned the pope was not Galileo's *science* but the way he *used* science to attack the Catholic Church's philosophy, which it had adapted from Aristotle.

You see, Aristotle offered a comprehensive philosophy covering not only metaphysics and ethics but also biology, physics, and astronomy. When Galileo built the first telescope and aimed it at the heavens, he discovered that Aristotle was dreadfully mistaken in his astronomy. For example, Aristotle taught that the sun was perfect, but Galileo discovered sunspots and other "imperfections."

Soon Galileo was attacking *all* of Aristotle's philosophy. He hoped to replace it with a new mechanistic philosophy that treated the world as a vast machine operating solely by mathematical laws, with God as the Great Mechanic.

That's when Catholic authorities got worried. They saw clearly that Galileo was not just addressing scientific questions but was instead attacking Aristotelianism as an entire system. But Aristotle taught a classical view of ethics that many theologians appealed to in defending biblical ethics. They were afraid that Galileo's scathing attacks could destroy the moral basis for the social order.

It was this concern for morality and social order, not hostility to science, that motivated the Catholic hierarchy to oppose Galileo. The conflict was not between religion and science per se but between Christians' holding different worldviews: the Aristotelian worldview adopted by the Catholic Church and the competing mechanistic worldview proposed by Galileo.

The fact is that Christianity itself is not inherently hostile to science. If it were, we would be hard pressed to explain why so many founders of modern science were Christians.

Some historians even speculate that science may never have developed were it not for Christianity. For example, science writer Loren Eiseley says that many civilizations developed great technical expertise—Egypt with its pyramids, Rome with its aqueducts—but only one produced the experimental method we call science. That civilization was Europe at the end of the Middle Ages—a culture steeped in Christian faith. Eiseley writes, "Experimental science began its discoveries . . . in the faith . . . that it was dealing with a rational universe controlled by a Creator who did not act upon whim." Again, the very idea that there are "laws" in nature is not found in any other culture.

Sociologist R. K. Merton says modern science owes its existence to biblical moral obligation. Since God made the world, Christians have taught that we have an obligation to study it and use it to the glory of God and for the benefit of humanity. Once again, God's instructions for the first humans to name the animals and exercise dominion over all creation are intrinsic to life's purpose.

Eiseley and Merton are not Christians. Yet they are expressing a consensus among historians that Christian faith actually propelled the development of modern science.

It's true that God himself can't be put in a test tube or studied under a microscope. But it is God who created and sustains the natural laws that scientists appeal to in their theories. And scientists who reject Christian faith are actually cutting off the branch they're sitting on.

> *God, who founded everything in the world according to the norm of quality, also has endowed man with a mind which can comprehend those norms.*
>
> Johannes Kepler, quoted in *The Soul of Science*

It's time for Christians to stop being defensive about our history. Don't sit passively when you hear these old charges that Christianity is an enemy of science.s

The history of science is largely a story of *Christians* debating how to understand God's relationship to the world. Whether it's Galileo on the Leaning Tower of Pisa or Newton with his apple, Western science has a rich history of Christians' putting their faith into action.

Q 29: *If there is life on other planets, does that mean Christians are all wrong about God?*

In 1996 NASA scientists announced that they might have found evidence of life from Mars: organic molecules embedded in a meteorite found in Antarctica. The media instantly went into orbit, and even the president hailed the discovery as significant.

The reason for all the hoopla is that life on other planets has been long considered potential confirmation of the naturalistic worldview—the theory that life arose by purely natural forces. Science journalist Timothy Ferris argues in *The New Yorker* that if organisms existed on Mars, then "life, far from being a singular miracle" on Earth, may in fact be the predictable consequence of certain planetary conditions. Life on Mars, Ferris argues, would prove that life starts "routinely," whenever conditions are right on Earth, Mars, or anywhere else.

In other words, if martian life did exist, some interpret that as tipping the balance in favor of naturalism instead of a Creator.

But would life on other planets really prove there is no God? Not at all. No matter where life is found, it is more complex than anything produced by known natural forces. Finding new forms of life in strange places doesn't change that fact.

Imagine you were from a Stone Age culture and saw a computer for the first time. You would have no idea where such a complex structure came from. If someone handed you a second computer, would that tell you where computers come from? Of course not. No mystery was ever solved by adding a second mystery.

In the same way, if the origin of life on Earth is a mystery, then finding life somewhere else does nothing to solve the mystery. The simplest living things are astonishing in their complexity. If life, even as tiny bacteria, existed on Mars, it would still be far beyond anything purely natural laws can explain.

Christians believe that wherever life occurs, it was created by a personal God. As biologist and philosopher Paul Nelson puts it, "The intelligent design claim is not that life is restricted to earth. It's that wherever life occurs, it's created by intelligence."

The Scriptures say nothing about whether life-forms exist anywhere else in the universe. Historically, many Christians have found it perfectly possible that life exists on other planets. In *God in the Dock,* C. S. Lewis wrote that the universe "may be quite full of life" and argued that we humans have no right to prescribe limits to God's interests. Of course, the molecules in the rock found in Antarctica may or may not really indicate traces of life. Many scientists remain skeptical, and this side of heaven, we may never know for sure whether life exists on other planets.

But wherever life exists, we can be sure of one thing: It was not the product of natural forces but of an intelligent Creator.

KEY POINTS IN BRIEF

✓ The question of whether God exists or nature is all there is remains a philosophical question, whether it is answered by scientists or theologians.

✓ The famous test-tube experiments on the origin of life have only proven how much intelligence it takes to approximate the origin of life. They have not by any means proven that life can come about by chance.

✓ Macroevolution—the gradual evolution of new species—has never been proven. The complexity and intelligent arrangement of DNA coding suggests macroevolution depends on a false theory.

✓ Evolutionists themselves insist that their theory leaves no place for God. Theistic evolution may well be an untenable compromise.

✓ Besides DNA coding, the anthropic principle and the irreducible complexity of living structures are evidences of intelligent design. It's relatively easy to distinguish naturalistic phenomena (such as waves pounding on the shore) from intelligently created phenomena (such as the pyramids of Egypt). The criteria we use to distinguish one from another can be applied to the origins of life.

✓ The "fact of evolution" is a powerful myth today and poses enormous challenges for thoughtful Christians, whether teenagers or adults.

✓ Christianity is largely responsible for the advent of modern science within Western culture. Christianity is not opposed to science; instead, it provides a fitting context for the investigations of science.

CHAPTER 4
Can We Really Believe the Bible?
Reason, Historical Evidence, and the Scriptures

Q 30: *Isn't the Bible like other ancient books, filled with myth and superstition?*

This shouldn't be an unexpected question because many voices within our culture are doing their best to foster this impression. During a recent Christmas season *USA Today* ran an article called "Who Was Jesus?" which portrayed the gospel as a collection of myths and legends. *Newsday* ran an article with a similar theme. So did the *Toronto Star* and even the conservative *U. S. News and World Report*.

Yet the media virtually ignored a much more interesting story that broke at the same time, a story that supports the Bible.

Within a few miles of Nazareth, where Jesus grew up, archaeologists have uncovered two cities that reveal a surprisingly advanced level of culture. Gently scraping away the dust of centuries, archaeologists uncovered jewelry, stoneware dishes, industrial olive presses, and a Roman amphitheater big enough to seat four thousand spectators. Scholars were amazed. Obviously Nazareth was no backwater village. It was situated in the middle of a cosmopolitan center of culture and commerce.

And Jesus' disciples were not ragged, rustic wanderers. They were small-business owners with considerable economic savvy, engaged in trade with far-off cities. Galilee, it turns out, was as sophisticated as any other part of the Roman Empire.

This is not the first time archaeologists have added to our historical understanding of the Bible. There was a time when critics said Moses could not have written the Pentateuch because writing hadn't been invented yet. Then archaeologists discovered that writing was well developed not only in Moses' day but even before Abraham. Centuries before Abraham was born, Egypt and Babylonia were filled with schools and libraries. Archaeologists have dug up dictionaries written in four languages, compiled for translators.

There was a time when critics cast doubt on the geography of the Bible. For example, once scholars referred to the Hittites as a mythological people mentioned only in the Bible. But today many museums display the massive stone statues characteristic of Hittite culture.

Critics once reserved their sharpest skepticism for the early chapters of Genesis, reducing the patriarchs to sheer legend. But today archaeology has shown that Genesis gives a highly accurate description of names, places, trade routes, and customs of patriarchal times.

In the words of British historian Paul Johnson, "Christianity, like the Judaism from which it sprang, is a historical religion, or it is nothing. It does not deal in myths and metaphors and symbols, or in states of being and cycles. It deals in facts."

It is not now the man of faith, it is the skeptic, who has reason to fear the course of discovery.

Paul Johnson, "A Historian Looks at Jesus"

Of course, there will always be critics. But the Bible, unlike other ancient books, continues to pass with high marks when its historical accuracy is tested. The Bible has been cross-examined and found reliable.

Q 31: *The Bible was written by so many people—how accurate can it be?*

Many people feel that errors were introduced into the Bible because it was copied and recopied so many times. This is such an important issue, particularly in regard to the New Testament.

Christianity depends on history. For this reason few questions have been more exhaustively and critically examined through the centuries than those about the accuracy of the Scripture.

My own study as a skeptical lawyer brought me to the following unexpected conclusions. The men who wrote the New Testament were Hebrews, and scholars agree that the Hebrews were meticulous in their precise and literal transcriptions. What was said or done had to be recorded in painstaking and faithful detail; if there was any doubt about a particular event or detail, the detail was not included.

Furthermore, to ensure the authenticity of the Bible, God made sure Christ's life was recorded from a variety of perspectives. Oddly enough, all of the accounts correspond, even Paul's, although he was not a follower of Christ during the Lord's earthly ministry.

New archaeological discoveries in the field of biblical studies have added weight to the evidence that the Gospels were written by Jesus' contemporaries who had firsthand knowledge of his life and the events of the early church. (We'll discuss these further in the next chapter.) There are more reasons than ever to believe that the Bible was faithfully transcribed and is historically accurate.

Q 32: *Why are people so skeptical about the Bible's accuracy?*

Skeptics often criticize Christians for having a hidden agenda, for seeing what they want to in the Bible. But that argument can be turned on its head. Perhaps the skeptics have their own hidden agenda.

In fact, most skeptical theories of Scripture were devised before archaeology had become a science. People became skeptics not because of the facts but because of their philosophy—strangely enough, the same philosophy that underlies Darwinism: evolution.

Long before Darwin developed evolution as a biological theory, it was already a philosophy. Nearly two hundred years ago the philosopher Georg Friedrich Hegel argued that everything moves in stages from simple to complex—including societies and ideas. No idea, he argued, is true in an absolute or timeless sense.

In the field of theology, Hegel's evolutionary philosophy led to what we call "higher criticism" and is at work today in projects like the Jesus Seminar. If ideas evolve, theologians decided, then religious ideas must begin with crude, simple notions about God and move gradually to more sublime notions.

The trouble is, the Bible doesn't show any such progression. It doesn't begin with "primitive" ideas, like animism and polytheism, and then progress to more "advanced" ideas, like monotheism. Instead, it reflects a high ethical monotheism right from the opening words of Genesis.

But that didn't stop the modernist theologians. We'll just figure out the "correct" evolutionary sequence, they said, and rearrange the Bible to make it fit. Passages that theologians regarded as crude they dated earlier, while passages they regarded as more refined they dated later—no matter where those passages actually appear in the biblical text.

The very fact that the Bible doesn't fit the evolutionary sequence, critics said, proves that it is full of errors.

> *The Bible is supported by archaeological evidence again and again. On the whole, there can be no question that the results of excavation have increased the respect of scholars for the Bible as a collection of historical documents.*
>
> Millar Burrows, quoted in *Bibliotheca Sacra*

Here is the root of biblical skepticism. It didn't stem from any difficulty in fitting the Bible to the historical facts of archaeology. It was purely an armchair effort to force Christianity into an evolutionary mold.

So when you hear the word *evolution,* don't just think of Darwin.

The most destructive part of evolution has been its philosophy—one that insists on forcing everything, even religion, into a preconceived evolutionary sequence.

And as archaeologists make new discoveries, they increasingly discredit the evolutionary philosophy.

Q 33: *What about the miracles? Were they real?*

When I talk about the historical truth of the Bible, people often ask, What about Jonah and the whale? What about Noah and the Flood? What about the parting of the Red Sea? These stories are held up as so preposterous that no one could possibly take the Bible seriously.

But scientists who study these events say they are not as impossible as they might seem. Sometimes they are just special cases of perfectly normal laws of nature.

Take, for example, the parting of the Red Sea. The biblical record says God used the east wind, blowing all night, to push the waters back. Now it's a well-known scientific fact that a steady wind blowing over a body of water can change the water level. So two oceanographers decided to see if the same thing could happen on the narrow sliver of the Red Sea reaching up into the Gulf of Suez, where many scholars believe the Israelites crossed as they were escaping from Pharaoh's army.

Writing in the *Bulletin of the American Meteorological Society,* the scientists concluded that a moderate wind blowing constantly for about ten hours could very well have caused the sea to recede a mile or two. The water level would drop ten feet, leaving dry land for the Israelites to cross. "The Gulf of Suez provides an ideal body of water for such a process because of its unique geography," said one of the scientists.

Later, an abrupt change in the wind could cause the water to return rapidly—in a sudden, devastating wave. It could easily have trapped Pharaoh's troops, just as the Bible describes.

The study doesn't prove that the crossing of the Red Sea happened exactly this way, of course. It merely shows that God could have used perfectly normal forces to perform his miraculous deliverance.

Now a skeptic might argue that if there's a natural explanation, then it wasn't a miracle after all. But if it was only a natural event, isn't it strange that the sea parted just when Moses held out his staff? And that it fell back just when Pharaoh's soldiers were in hot pursuit?

No, God may use a natural process to accomplish his goals, but it's still a work of his hand, in his timing, and for his purposes.

Sometimes the Bible even provides intriguing clues that take millennia to verify. In his book *An Anthropologist on Mars,* Oliver Sacks describes the case of a man named Virgil, who had been blind since childhood. At the age of fifty, Virgil underwent surgery to restore his sight.

What Virgil experienced afterward inadvertently confirmed the Bible's account of one of Jesus' miracles. Following the surgery, Virgil suffered from what is called post-blind syndrome: the inability to make sense of the panorama of colors and shapes that crowd our field of vision. As Sacks writes, Virgil would "pick up details . . . an angle, an edge, a color, a movement, but he would not be able to synthesize them, to form a complex perception at a glance." For example, when looking at a cat, Virgil "would see a paw, the nose, the tail, an ear, but he couldn't . . . see the cat as a whole."

It took time and practice, but Virgil studied a tree and finally learned to put it together. As his wife put it, "He now knows that the trunk and leaves go together to form a complete unit."

These words ought to ring a bell for Christians who know their New Testament. The story of Virgil bears an uncanny resemblance to the story of the blind man of Bethsaida.

Mark 8:24 says that upon being healed of his blindness, the man told Jesus, "I see people, but I can't see them very clearly. They look like trees walking around" (NLT).

In the *National Review,* D. Keith Mano notes that this phrase "is not a poetic image. It is a clinical description." This biblical healing describes the same phenomenon experienced by Virgil. In short, Mano concludes, "this is irrefutable evidence that a miracle did occur at

Bethsaida. . . . No [charlatan] in the crowd could have faked it all by pretending to be blind. . . . A faker, not knowing about post-blind syndrome, would have reported that Jesus had given him perfect vision."

Instead, the New Testament reports that Jesus cured the man twice: once of blindness and then of post-blind syndrome (see Mark 8:25).

In the age of science, skeptics and even some Christians are all too eager to explain away the miracles of Christ. They claim that advances in science will eventually provide a naturalistic explanation for what appear to be supernatural events.

But ironically, as Virgil's story shows, science is providing a wonderful apologetic for Christianity. The story of the blind man's miraculous healing by Jesus could not be understood until our own day, when modern medicine has given us additional information about the restoration of sight.

The incident of the curing of the blind man at Bethsaida not only concurs with our scientific understanding of sight but also attests to the burden the Gospel writers felt to get the details right—even those they didn't understand.

Q 34: *Do I have to believe the whole Bible? Can't I choose to believe the parts that I'm comfortable with or that work with my own philosophies?*

We live in a pick-and-choose world. Advances in technology allow us more freedom to live and work on our own terms, within our own comfort zones. With just a push of a button we can sign on or tune in to 1,001 sources of information, using what we want, discarding the rest. Why shouldn't we be able to zap through God's Word and choose what suits us, just as we might choose food in a cafeteria line?

Because when we use the pick-and-choose approach to the Bible to justify our own prejudices, the result is either disaster or a gospel deprived of its saving power. History is full of accounts of how God's sacred Word has been bent and reshaped and used as a mere tool to support people's own crusades and erring theologies. In the nineteenth century many Americans who supported slavery cited Bible verses taken out of context as justification of their viewpoint.

Unlike the harsh crusades of the past, today's crusade—this salad-bar approach—often seeks to use the Scriptures for no other purpose than to secure our own comfort zones.

One such "comfort zone" crusade is to recast Jesus to fit a modern secular perspective. It's growing, and theologians are leading the way. Just listen to some of the titles hitting the bookshelves. John Spong's *Born of a Woman: A Bishop Rethinks the Birth of Jesus* offers the preposterous suggestion that Mary was raped and that the Virgin Birth was concocted by the church as a cover-up.

In *Jesus the Man,* divinity professor Barbara Thiering writes that Jesus didn't die on the cross; he was just poisoned. He was revived and went on to marry and raise three children.

In *The Historical Jesus,* Catholic theologian John Crossan argues that Jesus didn't rise from the dead. Instead his body was buried in a shallow grave, Crossan says, where it was dug up and devoured by dogs.

Taken together, books like these can create a widespread climate of opinion that the Bible is simply a collection of myths and errors. Even evangelical Christians may gradually accept the same principle and begin to separate faith from facts. The Bible is true in its spiritual message, they say, but full of errors in its history.

But Scripture never separates faith from facts. In 1 Corinthians 15, Paul explicitly argues that if Christ was not physically raised from the dead, our faith is worthless. Further, Paul warns in the strongest possible terms against changing the gospel to suit our own purposes. "As we have said before," Paul writes, "so I say again now, if any man is preaching to you a gospel contrary to that which you received, let him be accursed" (Gal. 1:9, NASB).

Besides, once you accept in principle that Scripture can be wrong, you start performing surgery on the text. You sort out certain historical details and stack them in a pile marked "believable," label the rest "unbelievable," and dump them out. But surely this is illogical. It's all the same text. If the Bible is reliable on some facts, why does it suddenly become unreliable on others?

No, the Bible is not like a beanbag chair that is made to adjust to each individual. We must accept the Bible in its total message. Otherwise, all we're doing is remaking Jesus to fit our own personal prejudices.

KEY POINTS IN BRIEF

✓ The Bible is historically accurate. Archaeological evidence has disproved many objections that critics once made.

✓ We have every reason to believe in the accuracy of the New Testament texts. Most of the men who wrote the New Testament were Hebrews, and scholars agree that the Hebrews were meticulous in their precise and literal transcriptions.

✓ Skepticism about the Bible's accuracy arose because of Hegel's evolutionary philosophy, not because of empirical evidence. He taught that ideas evolve, and as a result theologians decided that religious ideas must begin with crude, simple notions about God and move gradually to more sublime notions. The Bible doesn't show any such progression. It reflects a high ethical monotheism right from the opening words of Genesis.

✓ Modernist theologians applied Hegel's evolutionary notions of the Scriptures, dating passages they regarded as crude earlier, and passages they regarded as refined, later. This underlies what came to be called "higher criticism" and is still at work in projects like the Jesus Seminar.

✓ The miracles of the Bible tend to be confirmed, rather than disproved, by scientific investigations.

✓ The Bible must be accepted as a whole. The Scriptures never separate faith from facts (see 1 Corinthians 15).

CHAPTER 5

Who Is Jesus Christ, and Why Does He Matter?
The Reality, Mission, and Work of Jesus Christ

Q 35: *How do we know that Jesus was even real? Maybe the disciples made him up.*

Because young people almost never talk about Jesus in school, they can easily get the impression either that he didn't really live or that if he did, he doesn't really matter.

We know that Jesus lived because we have historical accounts that were recorded a mere twenty to forty years after his crucifixion. That's within a single generation—less than the time separating us from the end of World War II—and far too brief a span for myths and legends to take hold.

In fact, if we compare the historical evidence for Jesus to the evidence for other figures who lived in ancient times, there's just no comparison. Consider this: Although we don't have the original documents of the New Testament, we do have several thousand copies— some of them written within a hundred years after Jesus lived.

Compare that to the evidence of several other writers. The Roman writer Tacitus is considered a first-rate historical source. Yet we have only twenty copies of his work, and the earliest manuscript is dated a thousand years after he lived. No one doubts the authenticity of the Greek philosopher Aristotle. Yet the earliest copy of his work is dated fourteen hundred years after he lived. We all know about Julius

Caesar. Yet the earliest copy of his *Gallic Wars* is dated a thousand years after the original.

There can simply be no doubt that the New Testament is an authentic document—that it describes real events. The fact of Jesus' existence is better authenticated than that of any other figure from ancient times. So when your teenagers or their friends ask if Jesus was a real person, respond with your own question: Was Julius Caesar a real person? Was Aristotle? If they say yes, tell them the evidence for Jesus is much stronger.

What is even more startling is that a German scholar has uncovered new evidence that three tiny scraps of Scripture that he found in an Oxford University library were written by a contemporary of Christ—a contemporary who had firsthand evidence that Jesus was the Son of God. The scraps contain lines from Matthew 26 and describe a woman's anointing of Jesus and Judas's betrayal of Christ.

The fragments were donated to Oxford's Magdalen College library in 1901 by a missionary alumnus who brought them from Egypt. And there they sat for nearly a century, until a German researcher named Carsten Thiede recently decided to take a closer look at them.

Earlier scholars believed the papyrus was written in the second century. But advances in research on Greek texts enabled Dr. Thiede to come to a different and more accurate conclusion. He realized that the fragments were written in a Greek script that was common in the first century B.C. but went out of fashion around the middle of the first century. He concluded that the Magdalen manuscript was actually written in about A.D. 50—a mere seventeen years after the crucifixion of Christ. And the Oxford manuscript is itself a copy, which means the original Gospel of Matthew must have been written even earlier.

If Dr. Thiede's findings hold up, it could mean that the Gospel of Mark, which predates Matthew's Gospel, was written as early as A.D. 40—only seven years after the crucifixion.

Think of it—only seven years!

Dr. Thiede's conclusions throw a real monkey wrench into the teachings of liberal scholars who contend that the Gospels were written a hundred years or more after Christ's crucifixion and that contemporaries of Jesus didn't believe his claims to divinity. They dismiss the accounts of his miracles and resurrection as products of the oral tradition.

> ***In no other case is the interval of time between composition of the book and the date of the earliest extant [existing] manuscripts so short as in that of the New Testament. . . . [It] becomes so small as to be in fact negligible, and the last foundation for any doubt that the scriptures have come down to us substantially as they were written has now been removed.***
>
> Sir Frederick G. Kenyon

But if the Gospels really were written shortly after Jesus walked the roads of Galilee, as evangelicals believe, then there wasn't time for a fanciful oral tradition to spring up. Even more exciting is the fact that when the Magdalen manuscript refers to Jesus, it uses the word *Lord,* translated from a Greek term that was reserved exclusively as a reference to God, proving that the earliest Christians did believe that Jesus was God himself.

Christians shouldn't be surprised when historical documents authenticate biblical truth. As historian Paul Johnson writes, "In the long term, Christian truth and historical truth must coincide."

Thanks to decades of liberal teaching, many people today aren't sure whether the New Testament is trustworthy. That's why these Magdalen fragments are so important. They provide solid evidence for the historicity of Scripture and bring the historical reality of Christ into sharper focus than ever before.

Q 36: *Wasn't much of the "historical evidence" for Christianity simply manufactured by Christians?*

No one has ever found any solid evidence to support this idea. The early Christians knew their faith was rooted in historical events, and external evidence continues to verify the historical accuracy of the Gospel accounts. The Gospels say that Jesus was tried before the high priest Caiaphas. When an ancient burial cave was excavated in Jerusalem in 1993, the tomb of the Caiaphas family was discovered. Inside were the very bones of the infamous high priest mentioned in the Gospels.

The Gospels note that Jesus was also taken to the procurator of Judea, Pontius Pilate; a first-century inscription discovered at Caesarea confirms that Pilate was procurator of Judea from A.D. 26–36.

What's more, the second-century Roman historian Tacitus confirms that Christianity was founded by a man named Christus, whom he says was "put to death as a criminal by Pontius Pilate, procurator of Judea, in the reign of Tiberius."

The most beautiful thing about Christianity is that if we had scholars spending their whole lives raising questions, in the end we'd only find more and more power in our tradition. We shouldn't be afraid of research.

James Charlesworth

Some people think that the holy places in Israel are just the product of pious legends. Through the years fervent pagans tried to cover up the roots of Christianity by building temples and other structures over them. But their efforts backfired. Instead of covering up the holy places of Christianity, they marked them for all time, giving powerful witness to the gospel records.

For example, in the year A.D. 135 the Roman emperor Hadrian had just subjugated Judea after the Second Jewish Revolt. Determined to impose Roman religion on the Judeans, he destroyed the Jewish synagogues in Jerusalem and then turned his attention to the Christians. What better way to squelch this upstart religion than to obliterate its holy places?

Christians at the time venerated the site of Christ's crucifixion and resurrection, so Hadrian concealed the site under a massive concrete platform and built a temple to the pagan god Zeus on top of it.

Nearly two centuries later the tables turned. When the emperor Constantine converted to Christianity, he wanted to build a magnificent church in Jerusalem to commemorate Christ's crucifixion and resurrection, and he *insisted* that the church be built on the actual site. When Constantine's architects arrived in Palestine, Christians pointed them to Hadrian's temple, which marked the very spot.

The builders set to work demolishing the pagan temple. Sure enough, underneath it they found the ancient quarry called Golgotha and nearby, the remains of the tomb of Christ. Today the Church of the Holy Sepulchre in Jerusalem's Old City still marks the site of the crucifixion and resurrection of Christ.

Christians built churches throughout the Holy Land to mark the location of actual historical events, not pious legends.

Q 37: *Jesus may have been a real person, but is he God?*

The essence of Christianity is summed up in one mind-boggling sentence: Jesus Christ is God (John 10:30).

Not just part of God . . . or sent by God . . . or related to God. He *is* God.

The more I grappled with those words when first considering the truth of Christianity, the more they exploded a lot of comfortable old notions I had floated through life with.

In C. S. Lewis's *Mere Christianity,* one of the most influential books in my conversion, he put it bluntly: For Christ to have talked as he talked, lived as he lived, and died as he died, he was either God or a raving lunatic.

These two alternatives present each of us with a choice—a simple, stark, and frightening one. Before reading Lewis's direct presentation of the only two real alternative views of Jesus Christ, I had been content to think of Christ as an inspired prophet and teacher who had walked the sands of the Holy Land. If one thinks of Christ as no more than that, I reasoned, then Christianity is like taking a sugarcoated placebo once a week on Sunday morning.

The leaders of Jesus' day did not seek his death because he was simply a good man (or a madman) or simply because he was a threat to their authority. Jesus was charged with blasphemy for claiming to be God (Mark 14:61-64). Jesus was executed because he claimed to be exactly who Christians today proclaim him to be—"very God of very God," in the words of the Nicene Creed.

Q 38: *What proves Jesus is God?*

Christ's bodily resurrection from the dead affirms Jesus' claim to be God. The Resurrection establishes Christ's authority and thus validates his teachings about the Bible and himself. As we alluded to earlier, the apostle Paul minces no words about this: "If Christ has not been raised, then your faith is useless" (1 Cor. 15:17, NLT).

Paul may be considered rash for staking the case for Christianity on the bodily resurrection. But Paul was absolutely certain about Christ's resurrection. He had encountered Jesus face-to-face on the road to Damascus and had talked both with the apostles who were with Jesus and with many of the five hundred eyewitnesses who saw the resurrected Lord (1 Cor. 15:6). The Resurrection resolves Jesus' claim to be Messiah and God.

Some people consider the Resurrection to be a hoax, the result of a conspiracy by Paul and the other apostles. As a former coconspirator in the Watergate scandal, I know the Resurrection could not possibly be a hoax perpetrated by a conspiracy or plot.

In March 1973, nine months after the infamous Watergate break-in at the headquarters of the Democratic National Committee, it was finally becoming clear to me and to Richard Nixon's other closest aides that there was a criminal cover-up and that the president could be involved. There were no more than a dozen of us who understood the seriousness of the situation. The question was, could we maintain the cover-up and save the president?

Consider that we were political zealots, among the most powerful men in the world. With all that at stake and with all our power, you would expect us to be capable of maintaining a lie to protect the president. But we weren't.

The human heart is singularly susceptible to fickleness, to change, to promises, to bribery. One of [the disciples] had only to deny his story under these inducements, or still more because of possible imprisonment, torture and death, and they would all have been lost.

Blaise Pascal, *Pensées*

The first to crack was John Dean, the aide who knew the most. He went to the prosecutors and offered to testify against the president. After that, everyone started scrambling to protect himself. Once that happened, the president was doomed; the conspiracy unraveled quickly. The great Watergate cover-up lasted only three weeks. We were some of the most powerful politicians in the world, and we couldn't keep a lie for more than three weeks.

What does this twentieth-century fiasco tell us about the first century? One of the most common arguments against Christianity is a conspiracy theory. Critics often try to explain the empty tomb by saying the disciples lied—that they stole Jesus' body and conspired together to pretend he had risen. The apostles then managed to recruit more than five hundred other people (1 Cor. 15:6) to lie for them as well, to say that they saw Jesus after he rose from the dead.

But how plausible is this theory?

To support it, you would have to be ready to believe that over the next fifty years the apostles were willing to be ostracized, beaten, persecuted, and (all but one of them) suffer a martyr's death without ever renouncing their conviction that they had seen Jesus bodily resurrected. Does anyone really think they could have maintained a lie all that time?

No, someone would have cracked, just as we did so easily in Watergate. There would have been some kind of smoking-gun evidence or a deathbed confession. But these men had come face-to-face with the living God. They could not deny what they had seen.

The fact is that people will give their lives for what they believe is true, but they will never give their lives for what they know is a lie. The Watergate cover-up proves that the twelve most powerful men in modern America couldn't keep a lie and that twelve powerless men two thousand years ago couldn't have been telling anything but the truth.

Q 39: *Why was it necessary for Jesus to die?*

We began answering this question in the chapter on the problem of evil. Jesus—God incarnate—"gave himself" (Gal. 1:4; Eph. 5:25) to bridge the gap and provide salvation for fallen, sinful humanity. In his death Christ took our sin on himself: "For God made Christ, who never sinned, to be the offering for our sin, so that we could be made right with God through Christ" (2 Cor. 5:21, NLT).

Let me quote a bit more from the apostle Paul: "All have sinned and fall short of the glory of God, and are justified [put right] freely by his grace through the redemption that came by Christ Jesus" (Rom. 3:23-24). Verse 26 says he "justifies [those] who [have] faith in Jesus."

We are asked to respond to the gift God gave us in Jesus' death and resurrection, to accept the truth of these events, and to call out to Jesus for his forgiveness and presence within our life.

To understand the response God asks of us, let's consider the scene of the Crucifixion itself. It presents us with five different kinds of people representing every possible response to Jesus. Each of us has to choose what kind of person he or she wants to be.

We can be like the guards who were casting lots for Jesus' clothes. A lot of people are trying to see what they can get from God.

Then there are those who laugh and sneer—like the leaders who mocked Jesus: "If you are the Christ, get yourself down off the cross." A lot of the world mocks Jesus today.

Most of the people at the execution watched with their hands in their pockets and did nothing. They're the saddest people of all. One can understand the people who were trying to get Jesus' clothes, and one can understand the mockers, but I can't understand the third kind of people, the ones who just stood by and watched, not caring as the Son of God was crucified for them.

There are two other kinds of people—represented by the thieves who died alongside Jesus. The first thief said to Jesus, "Aren't you the Christ? Save yourself and us!" (Luke 23:39). That's a universal human prayer: "God, get me out of here."

But that first thief didn't understand what the second thief understood. The second thief answered back: "No! Jesus is innocent, but we are getting what we deserve."

> *For God so loved the world that he gave his one and only Son, that whoever believes in him shall not perish but have eternal life. For God did not send his Son into the world to condemn the world, but to save the world through him.*
>
> John 3:16-17

This is one of the purest expressions of repentance in all Scripture. The Greek word for repentance is *metanoia,* which means a "change of mind." Repentance is the process by which we see ourselves, day by day, as we really are: sinful, needy, dependent people, and God as he is: awesome, majestic, and holy.

This thief's dying words to Jesus, "Remember me," are the classic statement of faith (Luke 23:42). With simplicity and power this man repented and believed. He died trusting in Christ and in the place Jesus promised him in paradise.

Jesus died for our sins—whether we are thieves on a cross or students in school. His death paid the debt we owe so that we do not have to face eternal death. He died so that we can choose life.

Q 40: *What about other religions that say there is one God? Aren't they just as good as Christianity?*

Muslims share our conviction that we can't explain existence naturalistically. But their revelation and their understanding of salvation is very different from ours. The Christian worldview alone offers the explanation of the human dilemma. *Alone.* Nothing but the atoning death and resurrection of Jesus Christ, God incarnate, provide the way out of the human dilemma.

If you compare worldviews (Marxism, naturalism, postmodernism, existentialism, Hinduism, Shintoism, Buddhism, Islam, Judaism, Christianity), you'll see this clearly. Muslims' only hope for redemption—that is, for deliverance from their own sinful condition—is their walk across a perilous sword of judgment after they die. If they slip off, they are lost.

Jews still await the coming of Messiah; they are without the promise that their sins have been forgiven.

Typical of Eastern thought, Hindus believe that in the next life someone will do to them what they have done to other people in this life. This belief simply perpetuates evil and keeps one in a hopeless and sinful condition.

Other Eastern religions promise cycles of life, or karma, also called the wheel of suffering, but in these faiths there is no hope, no promised redemption, no personal god to offer forgiveness.

Most of the New Age religions are merely adaptations of Eastern thought. Because people believe they are one with nature, they worship mother earth. The best they can hope for is some harmony or oneness with nature, becoming gods themselves. But this offers no sure hope, no assurance that we can be delivered from the great dilemmas of life.

All of the secular promises of deliverance have proven bankrupt. Some people said, for example, that releasing us from repressive influences, allowing us to live in sexual freedom, would actually be a form of redemption. Instead, it has delivered people into bondage.

Your teenager needs to know as we compare worldviews that the Christian understanding of reality is the only one that provides for a personal encounter with a living God who delivers us from our sins. It is also the only understanding of reality that conforms to the way things really are, that provides human dignity, that provides an explanation of where we're going and what our purpose is.

The apostle Peter says we should be prepared to give a reason for the hope that is within us but always with gentleness and reverence. As we talk with those who have other belief systems, we must always proclaim the singular truth of Christianity with love. We never lord it over others who don't share our beliefs. We ought to be patient and gentle toward those who don't have eyes to see or ears to hear the gospel.

Q 41: *What happens to people who die without ever hearing about Christ? It doesn't seem fair for them to go to hell.*

This question can take on real urgency for young people, especially when a young friend dies as the result of an illness or a tragic accident. But they will also hear this question as the first line of attack from those who insist that Christianity with its claims of salvation through Christ alone is simply unfair.

This is not really a question about the lost. The issue is much bigger than this. The real issue is whether God is going to be God on our terms or his. Let me explain.

Suppose we answered this question by saying, "Well, God doesn't hold accountable those who have never heard of Jesus. He'll find some other way of saving them, perhaps through the sincerity of their own beliefs." There are two serious problems with this answer.

First, it contradicts Jesus' claim that he alone is "the way and the truth and the life" and that "no one comes to the Father" but through him (John 14:6). The apostles also acknowledge that there is salvation in "no other name under heaven" than the name of Jesus (Acts 4:12). Either Jesus and the apostles are correct in their claims, or the whole framework of the Christian faith collapses in a heap at our feet.

Second, suppose we said that God won't judge those who have not heard. In that case, wouldn't it be the most loving thing a Christian could ever do to resolutely refuse to mention the name of Jesus to anyone? That way everyone would be saved, or at least we would not be the cause of anyone's hearing and rejecting the gospel and thus being condemned.

But this flies in the face of the great commission, our Lord's command to go and preach the gospel to all creation (Mark 16:15). The urgency of the great commission suggests that we must undertake this task whatever the cost and persist at it until the Lord returns at the consummation of history. In fact, throughout the ages this is exactly what the church has endeavored to do.

But in spite of this, some people will never hear the gospel. Is it fair for God to judge and condemn those people? We may answer this along two lines, each of them soundly based in Scripture.

First, the Bible tells us that every person possesses a basic knowledge of God (as we have previously discussed). God has so clearly revealed himself in nature and in the human conscience that people are without excuse before him (Rom. 1:20). But without excuse for what? For not having sought out more knowledge about him, for one thing. Paul says that one of the reasons God has revealed himself so clearly is that he intends for people to seek him so that they might find him as he shows more of his grace and truth to them (Acts 14:17; 17:26-27).

Tragically, many people turn away from God's clear revelation to make other gods for themselves. Indigenous peoples in remote cultures make idols of wood and precious metal, or they ascribe divine powers to rivers, clouds, and mountains. More "sophisticated" Western people put their faith in money, prestige, or sensual experience. Instead of seeking the God who is continuing to reveal himself to them—their rebellion against him notwithstanding—they pour their energies into all manner of false gods and embrace the ethics those gods inspire (see Romans 1:21-32). This leads them into ever deeper levels of sin and disobedience, the hardening of their heart toward God, and ultimately an attitude that says, "There is no God" (Ps. 14:1). Such an attitude cannot help but fall under the condemnation of the God of heaven and earth.

Rather more difficult to understand is what the Scriptures teach concerning the nature of salvation. The Bible tells us, "Salvation belongs to the Lord" (Ps. 3:8, NASB). No one deserves to be saved. All of us, because of our rebellion against God and our inclination toward sin, deserve to come under his eternal wrath. In a world of sinful people the fact that some are saved to glorious new life through Jesus Christ is a testimony to the greatness of God's mercy and grace.

Who will be saved? All who confess Jesus as Lord and believe in their heart that God has raised him from the dead (Rom. 10:9-11). But who will do that? All who hear the gospel and are given the gift of faith. Even the faith to believe the gospel is a gift of God's grace (Eph. 2:8-10). For our part, we must be faithful in proclaiming the message of God's love in Jesus Christ and calling our friends and neighbors to repentance and faith in him. But the ultimate disposition of salvation is in the Lord's hands.

Some people will ask, How can God still find fault? Since salvation belongs to him and he gives it to whom he will, how can he condemn those who have not heard? How can he condemn those who never hear? Paul's answer to the Romans when they asked that same question was essentially, "You can't ask that question" (Rom. 9:19-24). It is arrogance in the extreme to insist that God answer the question, that he explain his sovereign privilege and choice to fallen, sinful creatures so as to satisfy their fallen, sinful logic and sense of justice. " 'My thoughts are not your thoughts, neither are your ways my ways,' declares the Lord. 'As the heavens are higher than the earth, so are my ways higher than your ways and my thoughts than your thoughts' " (Isa. 55:8-9). In other words, there comes a place for trusting in the goodness and wisdom of God without having to understand in exhaustive detail why he does what he does. We simply have to resolve to be faithful to the great commission and leave to God the ultimate question about the people to whom he will show his mercy (Rom. 9:15-23). As the Scriptures assure us, "Will not the Judge of all the earth do right?" (Gen. 18:25).

KEY POINTS IN BRIEF

✓ The historical existence of Jesus is better authenticated than that of such figures as Tacitus and Aristotle from ancient times. We have no reason to doubt Christ's earthly life.

✓ New evidence from the Oxford University Magdalen College library suggests that the Gospel of Mark may have been written as early as A.D. 40, a mere seven years after Jesus' crucifixion. The new evidence also proves that the earliest Christians did believe that Jesus was God himself.

✓ Jesus claimed to be God, and he was executed for this claim.

✓ Jesus' resurrection proves he is God.

✓ People will give their lives for what they believe is true, but they will never give their lives for lies. All the apostles except one suffered martyrs' deaths, but they never renounced the bodily resurrection of Jesus. A conspiracy among Jesus' followers to lie about Jesus' resurrection for their own benefit is totally implausible.

✓ Jesus died for our sins. He wants us to ask for forgiveness and for his presence in our lives—as did the "repentant thief" crucified with him.

✓ Christianity alone presents the way for every person to be saved—to be restored to fellowship with God in Christ. Having said that, we must lovingly affirm the exclusive truth of Christianity as opposed to other religions.

✓ We must leave the ultimate status of every person's salvation to God, including those who never hear the gospel before their deaths. Our task is to go into the whole world and preach the Good News.

CHAPTER 6

What Does Becoming a Christian Mean?
The Life of Faith

Q 42: *Besides the promise of eternal life, what's so great about being a Christian? Aren't Christians fanatical and hung up on rules?*

Teenagers are not the only ones who have these concerns. Many people in our culture today try to stereotype Christians as wild-eyed zealots and legalistic Bible-pounding bigots.

Some even portray Christians as being mentally unbalanced. With his 1991 remake of the 1962 thriller *Cape Fear*, film director Martin Scorsese made one significant change: He turned the crazed villain into a Bible-quoting Pentecostal Christian with a cross tattooed across his back. In a scene in which the man tries to rape a woman, he shouts, "Are you ready to be born again?"

The message is clear: People who believe the Bible are deranged—and even dangerous. Scorsese was giving particularly dramatic expression to an assumption common in secular media and academia today: Religion is harmful to mental health. The idea goes back to Sigmund Freud, who regarded belief in God as a neurosis.

But in an interview in *Christianity Today*, Christian psychiatrist David Larson exposes that assumption as sheer myth. All through his psychiatric training, Larson says, he was repeatedly told that religious people are more neurotic. But when he examined the empirical data, he found exactly the opposite. He found that religious people are actually healthier than the general population, both mentally and physically.

For example, in reviewing the literature on the subject, Larson discovered that nineteen out of twenty studies showed religion playing a positive role in preventing alcoholism. And sixteen out of seventeen studies showed religion had a positive role in reducing suicide.

Religious commitment was associated with lower rates of mental disorder, drug use, and premarital sex. People who attend church regularly even show much lower blood-pressure levels.

One of the most striking differences Larson found is connected to divorce rates. Religiously committed people report much higher levels of satisfaction with their marriage and much lower rates of divorce. That, in turn, significantly reduces their incidence of divorce-related problems such as stress, depression, and even physical disorders.

In general, the empirical data show religious people are simply happier and better adjusted.

I have come that they may have life, and have it to the full.

John 10:10

Christians who live by God's revealed truth don't do so in order to deny life but to live it more fully. We believe our faith teaches us how to act in conformity with reality; we don't need to walk into the moral walls as if we were blind. This is part of God's grace to us. He gives us information about what kind of behavior makes for the most fulfilling life.

Crucially, we must always point out that a Christian isn't primarily concerned with obeying the rules: the Christian's first and last aim is loving the God who created our world. Out of love, we acknowledge who God is and what he has told us. Our happiness is a by-product of believing in God enough—of loving God enough—to trust what he tells us.

Despite the popular stereotypes, Christians aren't trying to impose their rules on others; we simply share the Good News so that others will find the same happiness and fulfillment that we experience in the Christian life.

Q 43: *Isn't Christianity just a religion for wimps?*

Nothing answers this question like stories of true heroism. Here are four from recent Christian history—a history that constantly impresses me with its wealth of such examples.

Half a century ago a young Lutheran pastor named Dietrich Bonhoeffer was involved in a failed plot to assassinate Adolph Hitler, and Bonhoeffer was executed by the Nazis for treason. Astonishingly, fifty-one years later Bonhoeffer was officially exonerated by a court in Berlin.

Bonhoeffer was not only a leader of the Resistance under the Third Reich but also a powerful voice for the church. In his book *The Cost of Discipleship,* Bonhoeffer paints a vivid picture of what it means to be true to the Christian faith under a hostile regime. Under persecution Bonhoeffer discovered that even though God's grace is freely given, it also exacts a high cost. He discovered "costly grace"—the call of God to what we might term Christian heroism.

It was costly grace that led Bonhoeffer to leave a safe haven in America and return to Nazi Germany so he could suffer with his fellow Germans.

It was costly grace that led Bonhoeffer to continue teaching and preaching the Word of God even though the Nazis tried to suppress his work.

Costly grace led Bonhoeffer to stand against a turncoat church that mixed Nazi doctrine with Christian truth. Along with other faithful believers, Bonhoeffer signed the Barmen Declaration, which boldly declared independence from both the state *and* a co-opted church.

Costly grace led Bonhoeffer to attempt to smuggle Jews out of Germany even though it led to his arrest.

Costly grace led this young pastor to set aside his commitment to pacifism and join the assassination plot against Hitler—which finally led to Bonhoeffer's execution by the Nazis.

Even in prison, Bonhoeffer's life shone with divine grace. He comforted other prisoners, who looked on him as their chaplain. He wrote many moving letters that were later collected in a volume called *Letters and Papers from Prison,* a book I read during my own stay behind bars, finding in it strength and encouragement.

On the morning of April 9, 1945—less than a month before Hitler was defeated—Bonhoeffer knelt, prayed, and then followed his captors to the gallows, where he was hanged as a traitor.

Today Bonhoeffer is finally receiving official recognition that matches the spiritual veneration he has inspired in so many believers. In Malcolm Muggeridge's book *The Third Testament* the late British journalist wrote a tribute to Bonhoeffer. "Looking back now across the years," Muggeridge wrote, "what lives on is the memory of a man who died, not on behalf of freedom or democracy or a steadily rising gross national product, nor for any of the twentieth century's counterfeit hopes or desires, but on behalf of a cross on which another man died 2,000 years before."

The lesson of Bonhoeffer's life and death is that God's grace demands everything—even our life—but in return it gives us a *new* life that transcends even the most oppressive political conditions.

Our second example also comes from World War II. When Adolph Hitler occupied Poland in 1939, he rounded up not only Jews but also all sorts of other "undesirable elements" who might oppose him. At the top of the list were Catholic priests.

And that's how Father Maximilian Kolbe, a gentle monk committed to evangelism, ended up in Auschwitz, the notorious Nazi concentration camp. It was a death camp: Jews were exterminated outright, and non-Jewish prisoners were worked to death.

In this place of despair, Father Kolbe brought hope to his fellow inmates. He heard their confessions, he prayed with them, he shared his meager rations with them. The prisoners, ragged and bone-thin, loved Father Kolbe; they saw in him the love of Christ.

But the real test came one summer morning in 1941, when the men from Father Kolbe's barracks were called out and ordered to stand in formation. The commandant screamed at them in fury. "An inmate has escaped!" he shrieked. "Escaped! And who will pay the price? You will. Ten of you will be sent to the starvation bunker."

The prisoners swayed in terror. Anything was better than the starvation bunker—death on the gallows, a bullet in the head, even the gas chambers. These were quick compared to a slow, excruciating death without food or water.

The commandant walked the rows, randomly choosing ten prisoners. One by one the men's camp numbers were written down. One by one they bowed their heads in despair. But one man couldn't hold back his agony. "My poor wife!" he cried out. "My children! What will they do?"

Suddenly a prisoner stepped forward.

"Halt!" cried the commandant. "What does this Polish pig want of me?"

The prisoners gasped. It was their beloved Father Kolbe.

The priest spoke softly. "I want to die in this man's place," he said, pointing to the prisoner sobbing for his family.

There was silence for a moment in the death camp of Auschwitz. The weeping prisoner, Bruno Borgowiec, stared in amazement. The other inmates held their breath. Then the Nazi commandant roughly pulled Kolbe from the ranks and allowed Borgowiec to return to his barracks.

The condemned men were taken to the starvation bunker. But something strange happened. Over the next few days, instead of hearing the usual screaming and moaning, all who came near the death cells heard the faint sound of singing. Father Kolbe led his flock through the valley of the shadow.

And in the end, he joined the Savior whose love he had shown so well.

Bruno Borgowiec, the inmate who had cried out for his family, was one of the few who survived Auschwitz. And he spent the rest of his life telling and retelling the story of Father Kolbe, the man who died in his place—who gave him a new life.

A third hero did not die for her faith; she lives it out year after year with great courage. Lady Caroline Cox of Queensbury, England, is on the board of Christian Solidarity International, an organization committed to humanitarian aid and human rights.

If you're picturing a well-dressed woman who does nothing but attend meetings, think again. Like the Energizer Bunny, Baroness Cox keeps going and going—straight into the world's deadliest danger zones.

For example, she's made two dozen trips to war-torn Karabakh, where 150,000 Christian Armenians are defending their land against seven million Muslims from Azerbaijan. On one of these trips Lady Cox's jeep was jolted by a rocket-propelled antitank missile. Her driver quit, but Lady Cox returned, bringing food, medicine, and Christian love.

She's done the same in southern Sudan, where millions of Christians have been persecuted, killed, or enslaved by the Islamic soldiers of northern Sudan. While other relief agencies were forced out, Lady Cox engaged in what she calls a little "unofficial drug running." In other words, she defied government policy, chartered planes, and flew in medicine—even bringing in a bishop so her brothers and sisters in Christ could celebrate at a service with the first clergy they had seen in years.

In Leningrad, Lady Cox investigated orphanages and helped rescue children living in inhumane conditions. Flying back to Armenia for the umpteenth time, the baroness visited a little boy blinded by shrapnel from a cluster bomb, and she wept with a nurse who had watched soldiers murder her son.

Lady Cox reminds us of Paul's message to the church at Corinth: When one part of the body of Christ suffers, all suffer. That brings us to the Christian definition of *heroism:* a willingness to suffer and sacrifice on behalf of others.

A fourth example is a brave teenager who risked his life to save a pastor from a denomination different from his own.

Laszlo Tokes, pastor of a small Hungarian Reformed church in Timisoara, Romania, preached the gospel boldly, and within two years membership had swelled to five thousand.

But success can be dangerous in a communist country. Authorities stationed police officers with machine guns in front of the church on

Sundays. They hired thugs to attack Pastor Tokes. They confiscated his ration book so he couldn't buy food or fuel. Finally, in December 1989, they decided to send him into exile.

But when police arrived to hustle Pastor Tokes away, they were stopped cold. Around the entrance to the church stood a wall of people. Members of other churches—Baptist, Adventist, Pentecostal, Orthodox, Catholic—had joined together to protest.

Although police tried to disperse the crowd, the people held their post all day and into the night. Then, just after midnight, a nineteen-year-old Baptist student named Daniel Gavra pulled out a packet of candles. He lit one and passed it to his neighbor.

Then he lit another. One by one the burning candles were passed out among the crowd. Soon the darkness of the December night was pierced by the light of hundreds of candles.

> ## *Christian heroism has not the same sources as heroism of other kinds. It has its source in the heart of God scourged and turned to scorn and crucified outside the city gates.*
>
> Jacques Maritain, *Freedom in the Modern World*

When Pastor Tokes peered out the window, he was struck by the warm glow reflecting off hundreds of faces. Here were members of the body of Christ, completely disregarding denominational divisions, joining hands in his defense.

The crowd stayed all through the night—and the next night. Finally police broke through. They bashed in the church door, bloodied Pastor Tokes's face, then paraded him and his wife through the crowd and out into the night.

But that was not the end. The people streamed to the city square and began a full-scale demonstration against the Communist government. Again Daniel passed out his candles.

First they burned for Christian unity; now they burned for freedom.

This was more than the government could tolerate. It brought in troops and ordered them to open fire on the crowd. Hundreds were shot. Young Daniel felt a searing pain as his leg was blown off. But the people of Timisoara stood bravely against the barrage of bullets.

And by their example they inspired the entire population of Romania. Within days the nation had risen up, and the bloody dictator Ceausescu was gone.

For the first time in half a century, Romanians celebrated Christmas in freedom.

Daniel celebrated in the hospital, where he was learning to walk with crutches. His pastor came to offer sympathy, but Daniel wasn't looking for sympathy.

"Pastor, I don't mind so much the loss of a leg," he said. "After all, it was I who lit the first candle."

The candle that was to light up the entire country.

What a powerful image—a black December night when the darkness was lit up by a glowing testimony to unity and freedom. A candle lit by a Christian teenager.

A faith for wimps? No. The lives of these four Christians—and countless more like them—show how challenging true Christianity can be. Living the faith nearly always presents a far greater challenge than mere rebellion. Often the Christian life takes a courage far beyond our own—courage only God can supply.

Q 44: *Christians say they are "saved," but why are some of them so mean and petty?*

Many a discussion has ended prematurely when parents, concerned to protect their beliefs, deny what anyone can see: there are a lot of Christians we wouldn't want to take a vacation with.

Sometimes Christians are mean. That's regrettable and inexcusable. And when we are, we disgrace the name of Christ.

I'm sometimes accused of being a hard-driving man. When I worked in the White House, it was said I would run over my own grandmother to get the president reelected. (While not literally true, the statement did reflect my attitudes.) But that was before I became a Christian. I know I am a different person today, with different values, goals, and sensitivities. God's grace has restrained me, and I hope my behavior reflects that.

Think of what we all would be like if God's grace did not restrain us. Several writers have helped put the matter in a clear perspective. Novelist Evelyn Waugh had a gift for making sharp comments that wounded even his friends. A woman once asked him, "Mr. Waugh, how can you behave as you do and still call yourself a Christian?"

Waugh replied, "Madam, I may be as bad as you say. But believe me, were it not for my religion, I would scarcely be a human being."

Christianity doesn't make people perfect. But it does make us better than we would have been without it. Remove the restraint of God's law, and the worst barbarism breaks forth.

C. S. Lewis put it this way: A crotchety old woman may be considered a poor witness for Christian faith. But who is to say how much more cantankerous she might be if she were not a Christian? And who is to say how much better a gentle, pleasant unbeliever might be if he *were* a Christian?

Despite Christians' faults, Christianity and God's grace have made the world and the people in it better than they would have been without them.

Q 45: *So how do I become a Christian?*

That's the best question of all! And I praise God for teenagers with the courage to ask it and for parents who lead them to see its decisive importance.

There are many ways to start answering this question. But by far the best, I think, is to share your own story with your teenager. Of course no two stories are the same, but one's own personal testimony can open doors to further discussion. Ask the Lord to open your son's or daughter's ears through stories of transformation in your own life or the life of someone else. You may be familiar with the story of my own conversion, but here I tell it briefly again, as I told it in my first book, *Born Again*.

I had been counsel to President Nixon, one of the most powerful positions in our nation, but in the summer of 1973 I found my world collapsing in the midst of the Watergate scandal. Tom Phillips, a friend and businessman, had told me of his conversion to Christ. I was impressed by the difference I saw in his life, and I decided to seek him out so that he could tell me what had really happened to him.

The crucial moment came one gray, overcast evening when I visited Phillips at his home. He read aloud the chapter on pride from C. S. Lewis's *Mere Christianity*. That one chapter ripped through the protective armor in which I had unknowingly encased myself for forty-two years. Of course, I had not known God, I realized as he read. How could I? I had been concerned with myself. I had done this and that. I had achieved. I had succeeded. In those brief moments while Tom read, I saw myself as I never had before. And the picture was ugly.

"Would you like to pray together, Chuck?" Tom asked, closing his Bible.

Startled, I emerged from my deep thoughts. "Sure—I guess I would—fine." I had never prayed with anyone before except when someone said grace before a meal. Tom bowed his head. "Lord," he began, "we pray for Chuck and his family, that you might open his heart and show him the light and the way."

As Tom prayed, something began to flow into me—a kind of energy. Then came a wave of emotion that nearly brought tears. I fought them back. It sounded as if Tom were speaking directly and personally to God, almost as if he were sitting beside us. Later, outside in the darkness, the iron grip I had kept on my emotions began to relax. Tears welled up in my eyes as I groped in the darkness for the right key to start my car. Angrily I brushed away the tears and started the engine.

As I drove out of Tom's driveway, the tears flowed uncontrollably. I was crying so hard that I pulled to the side of the road.

I forgot about pretenses, about fears of being weak. And as I did, I began to experience a wonderful feeling of release. Then came the strange sensation that water was not only running down my cheeks but surging through my whole body as well, cleansing and cooling as it went. They weren't tears of sadness and remorse, or even of joy; they were tears of relief.

And then I prayed my first real prayer: "God, I don't know how to find you, but I'm going to try! I'm not much the way I am now, but I want to give myself to you." I didn't know how to say more, so I repeated over and over these words: *Take me.*

That next week, away on vacation with my wife, I studied the book *Mere Christianity,* which my friend had given me, and I wrestled with the great questions. *Did I need to "get saved"? Did I need to be "born again"? Was Jesus really God?* The curious phrase "accept Jesus Christ" at first had sounded to me both pious and mystical, the language of the zealot, maybe black-magic stuff. But after my evening with Tom Phillips, I knew I could not sidestep the central question placed squarely before me.

Was I to accept, without reservations, Jesus Christ as Lord of my life? It was like a gate before me. There was no way to walk around it. I would step through, or I would remain outside.

"To accept" means no more than "to believe." Did I believe what Jesus said? If I did, then I accepted.

There was nothing mystical or weird at all, and there was no middle ground left. Either I would believe, or I would not. And I would believe it all or none of it.

It was Friday, at the end of a week spent in Maine searching for God and truth. As I pondered the week, my quest was not quite as important as I had thought. It simply returned me to where I had been when I asked God to "take me" in a moment of surrender on a little country road. What I studied so intently all week opened wider the new world into which I had already taken my first halting, shaky steps.

And so early that Friday morning, while I sat alone staring at the sea I love, words I had not been certain I could understand or say fell naturally from my lips: "Lord Jesus, I believe you. I accept you. Please come into my life. I commit it to you."

With these few words came a sureness of mind that matched the depth of feeling in my heart. God filled the barren void I had known for so many months, filling it to its brim with a whole new kind of awareness.

If your teenager has never prayed such a prayer and finds himself or herself without a genuine sense of belief, invite your teenager to do so. What a wonderful moment to share together. You gave your child life. Now give that child the opportunity to find eternal life in Christ.

Q 46: *I prayed the prayer. Now what's changed about me?*

When we surrender our life to the lordship of Jesus Christ, the God of the universe comes to live within us in the person of the Holy Spirit. We become his "home," and we are members of his kingdom, heaven's sentries here on earth.

At first we may not feel all that different, though. We have established an intimate relationship with God, pledging to be God's friend and helper. He may need to change us in many ways before we can be of great use. C. S. Lewis spoke of how new Christians often look for a few simple improvements—a redecorating or refurbishing of the soul. What they may come to experience, however, is a wholesale rebuilding program: God converting a shack into his own mansion.

Perhaps the process of conversion and "sanctification" (becoming that mansion God wants us to be) can best be seen in an individual life.

The great revival hymn "Amazing Grace" may be the only Christian hymn to find its way into the counterculture. Everyone from folksinger Joan Baez to Jimi Hendrix to today's rappers have arranged and recorded this spiritual classic.

The hymn's popularity would no doubt have surprised its composer, John Newton. For the circumstances that inspired him to write the hymn more than two hundred years ago were quite different from anything you or I have experienced.

Newton was a mere boy when he went to sea on his father's ship. As a young man, he reveled in a life of great debauchery. His duties included helping to capture West Africans and transporting them to the West Indies to be sold on the auction block. The unspeakable horrors of slavery evidently did not bother Newton, for he quickly rose to become the captain of his own slave ship.

Then, on a voyage from Africa to England in 1748, God's grace intervened. A terrible storm arose. As the fury of the waves threatened to capsize the ship, Newton searched the bookshelves of his cabin for something to take his mind off his fear. He snatched up a copy of *The Imitation of Christ,* the classic Christian devotional by Thomas à Kempis, a fifteenth-century Dutch monk. The sea eventually grew calm, but the experience changed John Newton forever. As Kenneth Osbeck writes in his book *One Hundred and One Hymn Stories,* "The message of the book and the frightening experience at sea were used by the Holy Spirit to sow the seeds of Newton's eventual conversion."

Yet Newton continued as captain of the slave ship for several more years. He attempted to justify his way of life by improving conditions aboard ship and even by holding religious services for his crew. But over time he realized that these gestures were not enough, that slavery itself is abhorrent to God.

Finally Newton left the slave trade for good and became a powerful crusader against slavery, joining forces with the great abolitionist William Wilberforce. The former sea captain was ordained an Anglican minister in 1764, and over the next forty years he wrote hundreds of hymns. It is believed that the melody Newton used for "Amazing Grace" was a West African chant that he had heard rising up from the ship's hold on one of his voyages as a slave trader. How supremely appropriate.

John Newton, the former slave-ship captain, knew well "how sweet the sound" of God's grace is—for he was painfully aware that he "once was lost" before God found him, that he "was blind" before God made him see.

Not long before he died at the age of eighty-two, Newton exclaimed, "My memory is nearly gone, but I remember two things: that I am a great sinner and that Christ is a great Savior!"

Like John Newton, the new Christian has embarked on a lifelong journey of growing into the likeness of his or her Lord—becoming more like Jesus day by day. In conversion we ask the Lord to dwell in our life and make it his own. He is a tremendously patient and gracious Lord, who over time will form and transform the convert. Listen to your conscience. Begin reading the Bible and praying daily. Ask Christ for assistance to quit destructive habits and other behaviors that make your life an unsuitable place for God's presence. This is a lifetime task.

Q 47: *But I can't remember when I didn't believe. Is that wrong?*

New life in the Spirit is conceived in the secret place of the soul, hidden from human eyes.

Many evangelicals believe that a person must know the precise moment he or she prayed "the sinner's prayer," must be able to recount that dramatic experience of "accepting Christ." In my life, as I've just recounted, God intervened powerfully in a moment I will never forget. Witnessed to by a faithful friend and humbled by the Spirit, in a flood of tears I surrendered my life to Jesus Christ.

For others, it's not that way. After my much-publicized conversion, Christian brothers and sisters would swarm around my wife, Patty, whenever she accompanied me to public events. "And when were you born again, Mrs. Colson?" they would ask, eager for another gripping conversion story.

At first this drove Patty to tears. "I don't know," she would reply. "All I know is I believe deeply."

Her pursuers would shrink away, and more than once they were heard to say, "Poor Mr. Colson. His wife isn't born again." But Patty, like millions of others, cannot pinpoint a precise moment or sudden awakening. She grew up in a Christian home, always attended worship services, and can never remember a moment when she didn't believe. She grew into faith in a quiet but very real way. After my conversion, Christ became intensely personal to both of us, the center of our marriage. Patty has experienced an ever-deepening relationship with Christ.

Later we found out that Patty is in some very good company: Ruth Bell Graham, wife of Billy Graham, came to Christ almost imperceptibly over time, in the context of a Christian home.

To pass from estrangement from God to be a son of God is the basic fact of conversion. That altered relationship with God gives you an altered relationship with yourself, with your brother man, with nature, with the universe. You are no longer working against the grain of the universe; you're working with it. . . . You have been forgiven by God and now you can forgive yourself. All self-hate, self-despising, self-rejection, drop away, and you accept yourself in God, respect yourself, and love yourself. . . . You begin to move toward others in love.

E. Stanley Jones, *Conversion*

The wind of the Spirit blows where it wills. We hear the sound, and we see the evidence, but we do not know how this mysterious breath of God touches human hearts.

If your teenager is able to say "Jesus is Lord" with real understanding and conviction, you don't need to introduce unnecessary anxiety by trying to pinpoint the moment when this belief became a reality. You probably did a better job than you knew as you faithfully instructed your child in the basics of the Christian faith.

Q 48: *How can I know God's will for my life?*

This question is both easy and hard to answer.

The easy answer is, God has made his will for us known in the Scriptures. The Bible is "a lamp to [our] feet and a light for [our] path" (Ps. 119:105). It is God's inspired revelation that is able to equip us for every good work in life (2 Tim. 3:15-17). It makes sense, therefore, that we who love the Lord and want to please him should seek to understand as much as we can of what he has revealed to us in his Word.

Still, we often struggle with particular choices. Should I date this person or that one? What should my major be? For what kind of career am I suited? Where should I go to college? These are not questions directly related to obeying or disobeying some clear revelation from God. Rather they are questions that require us to draw closer to the Lord and to use the resources he has put at our disposal for discerning his specific leading in our life.

But what are those resources?

First, prayer. Few decisions are so urgent that we have to make them on the spot. Most, such as the ones suggested above, can be taken to the Lord in prayer, honestly opened and deeply explored with him, until he touches our heart one way or another and leaves us at peace about our decision (see Philippians 4:6-7).

Second, mentors and models. Young people need to learn to look to those who are wiser than they. This is a discipline that will serve them all their years. If we can provide them examples of caring, wise, and approachable adults—parents, pastors, elders, teachers, neighbors, and so forth—who know the Lord, whose walk with the Lord makes them the kind of people teenagers can trust, then they will turn to such people in their times of decision making for advice and guidance.

Third, the Holy Spirit's leading. Teach your children how to "listen" for the leading of God's Spirit. I'm not suggesting that they will hear a voice or some new special revelation from God. Rather, once a decision has been made, they may find various kinds of confirmation of that decision or various obstacles to implementing it. These confirmations or obstacles will help them to know if this is really what God wants them to do. Paul experienced something like this as the Holy Spirit was working to change his mission plan and get him over to Greece (see Acts 16:6-10).

No special guidance will ever be given about a point on which the Scriptures are explicit, nor could any guidance ever be contrary to the Scriptures.

Hannah Whitall Smith, *The Christian's Secret of a Happy Life*

By continuing to grow in their understanding of God's Word, and through prayer and the advice of trusted counselors, young people can learn to distinguish God's will from the siren voices of the world when it comes to the difficult and important decisions they must make.

KEY POINTS IN BRIEF

✓ In general, the empirical data show that religious people are simply happier and better adjusted, have better marriages, less stress and depression, and even fewer physical disorders.

✓ Christians are primarily concerned with loving God, not with obeying the rules.

✓ Far from being a religion for the fearful, Christianity has called many to display heroic courage like that shown by Dietrich Bonhoeffer, Father Maximilian Kolbe, Lady Caroline Cox, and teenager Daniel Gavra.

✓ Christianity doesn't make people perfect. But it does make us better than we would have been without it.

✓ Sharing our own story of conversion with our children is the first way to begin talking about how to become a Christian.

✓ To become a Christian, we must confess our sin to Christ, confess belief in Christ's sacrifice and resurrection, and ask Jesus to take away our sins and come to live in our heart. A sample prayer might be: "Lord Jesus, I believe you. I accept you. Please come into my life. I commit it to you."

✓ The new Christian may not feel greatly changed. The work of Christ in the individual, however slowly it may proceed at first, inevitably brings about far-reaching changes that, with the believer's cooperation, make the soul capable of receiving to an ever greater degree the life of Christ.

✓ Even if a person has not had a spectacular, point-in-time conversion experience, the ability to say "Jesus is Lord" with understanding of what that means and with conviction confirms that a person has come into relationship with Christ. Many children raised in Christian homes grow into the faith gradually and almost imperceptibly.

✓ God's will for the believer is known chiefly through the Scriptures. Individual choices among competing options (choices that are not about right and wrong) are best guided by prayer, the counsel of mature Christians, and sensitivity to life circumstances that the Holy Spirit uses as signs confirming or redirecting our decisions.

PART II
WHAT SHOULD I DO ABOUT...?

CONTEMPORARY ISSUES AND
YOUR TEENAGER

CHAPTER 7

Why Do Christians . . . ?
Untangling Common Misconceptions

Q 49: *My friends say that Christians are always trying to impose their morality on others. Why shouldn't people make their own decisions about what's right and wrong?*

This question refers to our discussion about science and the nature of the universe. Because many people today believe the universe came about by chance, they also believe that human ethics cannot be governed by anything but pure choice. My values are simply what I choose to believe in—what I want to believe in or what I like to believe in.

Sociologist Robert Bellah says that Americans today are characterized by what he calls radical individualism. In his book *Habits of the Heart,* Bellah describes a survey of more than two hundred average, middle-class Americans. He discovered that in most cases their philosophy of life goes no further than individual gratification.

It's not that Americans don't care about others. Many of the people Bellah interviewed are firmly committed to their marriages, families, and communities. But when Bellah asked them why they care, all they could talk about was personal preference—"I feel comfortable doing this." "It makes me feel good." "It seems right to me."

Many people have no wider framework of what is true or what is real on which to base their moral choices. They have given up a notion of ethics based on something bigger than themselves and their own feelings.

One television interviewer seemed intrigued by the account of my conversion to Christ. But when we got to the subject of ethics, he looked at me quizzically and asked, "Do you have to be a Christian to be good? I mean, can't an atheist be good, too?"

I paused for a moment and then said, "Atheists can be good, but not consistently—only on impulse. Atheists have no objective reason for being good, no objective standard to guide them."

When moral commitments have no basis beyond personal impulse, they are very precarious. Feelings can be changing, contradictory, especially in the tumultuous years of adolescence. Which impulse should a teenager follow? How does the teenager know which impulse is right? Ethics based on pure choice makes for inconsistent and often poor behavior. That's the pragmatic answer to the question of why people shouldn't simply choose what's right and wrong for themselves.

The larger answer goes back once again to our belief in a created universe. Because God made the universe and humankind, both the world and human beings have an objective reality. Biblical standards of right and wrong are based on these realities—they teach us how to live in conformity with reality. They give us an objective standard for ethical behavior.

The great Russian writer Alexander Solzhenitsyn says that the line between good and evil is drawn not between principalities and powers but through every human heart. If people believe that all that matters is what feels right, they have no means to disarm the evil within them and to do good.

Having a firm conviction that ethical principles are not just the creation of my own mind and feelings makes those principles compelling. If I am good only because I want to be, I might just as well be *bad* because I want to be.

Q 50: *But isn't it judgmental for Christians to say that a person's feelings aren't legitimate?*

Everyone's emotions are no doubt real enough as emotions. But they are not the basis for morality. Morality is not a matter of personal feelings. Christians, because of our calling to love our neighbors, scannot abdicate our responsibility to point out that moral choices must be based on a shared reality—not on a person's private emotions.

As we've said, most Americans today cannot even see the difference. Sadly this applies to Christians as well as non-Christians.

Look at the abortion question, for example. Most people cannot explain their position beyond their own feelings on the matter. When Christian sociologist James Davison Hunter interviewed people for his book *Before the Shooting Begins,* he discovered that most Americans base their moral beliefs entirely on private feelings.

Take a young man named Scott, a former Catholic. Scott argues fiercely that the fetus is a human being, yet he insists that abortion should be legal. Why? The fetus is a person to me, Scott says, but it "might *not* be a person to that mother."

What Scott fails to see is that personhood is an objective fact: The fetus either is or is not a person, regardless of what you and I think or feel. But Scott is typical of many Americans who base their moral views on sentiment, not conviction.

When Hunter asked an architect named Paul why he supports the right to abortion, Paul became agitated. "I don't want to get into philosophical or theological wrangling," he said. "My feelings are based on experiences that are mine alone, and you can't tell me they are wrong."

Notice how Paul backs off from any objective discussion of abortion based on philosophy or theology, even at the most elementary level. Instead, he treats private experience as the final court of appeal. You know, if Paul ran his architectural firm the way he makes moral decisions, if he based his construction blueprints on sheer feelings, his buildings would collapse. To be a good architect, Paul treats physical facts with respect. They govern the practice of his profession. But he has no such respect for moral laws because he believes there are none.

When we separate facts and values, genuine moral debate becomes impossible. If morality is merely a matter of private feelings, then people perceive our attempt to reason with them as a personal attack.

A young mother named Karen told Hunter that she would never dream of getting an abortion herself, yet she could not bring herself to say that abortion is morally wrong for everybody. "I don't know how [other people] feel," she said defensively. Apparently Karen's greatest fear is that if she says abortion is wrong, she will hurt someone's feelings.

The majority of Americans, Hunter discovered, are just like Karen: pro-life in their personal lives yet pro-choice politically. Many are even hostile to the organized pro-life movement because in their words, pro-life activists "are trying to impose their views on everyone else."

But it is not "imposing" to express moral conviction. We can respect other people's feelings and still point out, in all charity, that there are objective standards and that we must decide great moral questions on the basis of those standards. Western civilization has been governed by a well-established tradition, a moral consensus based on biblical revelation. When our country's founders talked about "the laws of Nature and Nature's God," they were referring to this tradition, this understanding of moral truth respected by the people throughout the centuries. It is only in recent years that we have begun to challenge the objective reality of "Nature and Nature's God."

> *There is no such thing in the world as liberty, except under the law of liberty; that is, the acting according to the essential law of our being—not our feelings which come and go.*
>
> George Macdonald, *God's Word to His Children*

As parents we must constantly respect the feelings of our children—their anxieties about everything from the toddler's fear of the dark to the teenager's fear of marriage and family life—without agreeing that these feelings are based in reality. Making judgments about moral questions and talking with our neighbors or our teens about these questions demand exactly the same type of response.

Q 51: *But shouldn't we be tolerant of what others believe?*

Tolerance is often exalted as chief among democratic virtues. But what is the true nature of tolerance? And how far should it extend?

A recent Smithsonian expedition special on television pushed tolerance to absurd conclusions. The program highlighted a New Guinea tribe called the Korowai, a tribe that had never before been the subject of a study. The program presented the Korowai as enlightened people living in harmony with their environment.

Oh yes, they also happen to practice cannibalism.

Paul Taylor, a curator of the Smithsonian's National Museum of Natural History, hosted the program. The narrative began by telling us that the goal of anthropology is to make local customs seem "logical, reasonable, rational, and understandable."

And that's just what Taylor was eager to do. He told viewers that the Korowai live in tree houses that can rise as high as a six-story building, which Taylor described as "a major architectural achievement for any place in the world." The Korowai also practice equal pay for women, which, Taylor said, "feminists in any country in the world would very much agree with."

Things get a little trickier when it comes to equal rights in other areas: for example, the question of who will be killed and eaten. The Korowai practice cannibalism not only against enemy tribes but also against their own people as punishment for serious crimes. Serious crimes for men include sorcery and murder. Women may be eaten for stealing bananas and other food.

The Korowai were happy to describe the ritual in detail. The victim is first bound and shot with arrows. The body is then carefully cut into six pieces while the people "have a good time and sing." Finally, they cook the pieces over the fire and eat them.

The program presented this gruesome ritual as something Western- ers should not condemn but rather try to "understand." Many things about the Korowai may seem baffling, the narrator said, "until they are seen from within."

Within Korowai society, we were told, cannibalism is not "mere violence"; instead it is a "well-functioning example of how a complete criminal justice system works." In fact, the title of the program was *Treehouse People, Cannibal Justice.*

In Taylor's zeal to make cannibals appear "reasonable" and "logical," he never mentioned whether they insist on a fair trial before condemning someone to the cooking pot. In fact, he carefully refrained from making any moral judgments about the practice at all.

The entire program was an exercise in cultural relativism—an effort to deny the existence of objective standards by which to evaluate the cultural practices.

Seen from "within" the Third Reich, the murder of six million Jews and gypsies looked "reasonable" and "logical" too. Seen from "within" Islamic fundamentalist societies, the laws forbidding women common human rights, such as the ability to apply for a driver's license, look "reasonable" and "logical" too. Seen from "within" the Confederacy, slavery looked like a pretty good deal all around.

Being tolerant of others' opinions doesn't mean granting the validity of those opinions. This is the problem with the term *multiculturalism* we hear used so often, particularly in schools and colleges. Of course it is correct to be respectful of other cultures and to be sensitive to cultural differences. But that doesn't mean that all cultures are morally equal. In India, for example, a widow is still occasionally burned on her husband's funeral pyre. In Brazil men still practice what is called machismo, which amounts to the abuse of women. We would not consider these practices humane, to say the least.

There is nothing wrong or intolerant about pointing out the moral superiority of Western culture in those areas in which biblical truth has leavened that culture. We must evaluate everyone's opinions and practices—yours, mine, and our neighbors'—by the light of Christ revealed in the gospel of truth.

Q 52: *Does that mean Christians are totally rigid?*

This is a frequent accusation. A Gallup poll found that 50 percent of Americans are worried about fundamentalism. And what worries them is that fundamentalists actually believe in moral absolutes.

Why does that send a chill down people's backs? Because they have confused belief in absolutes with absolutism—a rigid mentality that is inflexible, irrational, and hostile.

But there's a world of difference between *absolutes* and *absolutism*. It is critical that you make this point clear to your teens.

You see, every time you tack -*ism* onto a term, you change its meaning. Think of the word *individual*—a good word, suggesting each person's dignity and worth. But the word *individualism* denotes something altogether different—an egoistic mentality that puts each person's interests above everything else.

Think of some other examples: There's a huge difference between *material* and *materialism;* between *human* and *humanism;* between *feminine* and *feminism.* So Christians ought to be bold in maintaining the reality of the existence of absolutes. But that doesn't mean we are absolutist in our mentality. A belief in absolutes simply means that we believe there is a created order—a source of truth. Truth is not something we agree on; it is something we discover. It is truth because it is reality, the way things actually are.

Moreover, we believe that there are virtues—like courage, fortitude, and patience—that are morally obligatory. We believe that there are normative patterns for marriage, business, and government. In short, we believe that there are laws for human behavior just as there are laws for the physical world.

Believing these things doesn't make you an absolutist any more than believing in gravity does. And if I try to persuade you of a moral law, I'm not "imposing my views" any more than I am if I teach you about the effects of gravity.

If we demonstrate a loving and patient attitude while we are talking to our teenagers about this, we will prove by our actions that believing in absolutes doesn't make us absolutists.

Q 53: *Then why do people see Christians as bigots?*

No group in America today is more the target of harsh stereotyping than what the media labels the Religious Right. But a look at the facts should make these negative stereotypes crumble. In 1992 George Gallup published one of the most significant studies ever done on Christians. Titled *The Saints Among Us*, it found that people with a strong Christian faith are happier, more generous in helping others, and—here's the real surprise—more tolerant.

The survey asked questions such as, "Would you object to the idea of a person of another race moving in next door?" Of the highly religious, 84 percent said they would not object, compared to only 63 percent of the nonreligious. The religious respondents also scored higher on related virtues such as compassion and forgiveness.

So much for the stereotype of intolerant hatemongers.

If the evidence contradicts the stereotype, why is it still so widespread? To begin with, Gallup's findings apply only to people highly committed to the Christian faith—about 10 percent of the population. Average churchgoers show little difference from the general population. So when non-Christians peer through the doors of the average church, they often see people whose lives demonstrate little of God's transforming power. These non-Christians don't get an accurate impression of Christianity's positive effects on the people who sincerely practice it.

Society condemns Christians as being intolerant for a second reason: Our culture has a distorted view of what true tolerance is. Americans tend to define tolerance as moral neutrality—refusing to judge any behavior as right or wrong. The classic definition of tolerance, however, is based on judgment: It means putting up with people precisely when we believe they are wrong. It means respecting all viewpoints, not silencing debates as today's politically correct strictures do.

The classic definition of tolerance stems from a Christian sense of sin and error. Since everyone falls short at some point, we are enjoined to tolerate people's shortcomings as long as they do not pose serious threats to communal life—while lovingly seeking to persuade them of the truth.

Real tolerance is a Christian virtue, and the evidence shows that it is Christians who practice it best.

The following personal encounter might provide some insight about our discussion of moral judgments and tolerance. I think the story reveals the culture's common assumptions about Christians and the real divide that exists between those who believe in an objective moral order and those who don't. The story illustrates just how hard it is for secular people—or our own teenagers who are steeped in secular culture—to understand the Christian point of view.

I was on *Nightline* at the time of the twentieth anniversary of the Watergate break-in. (I realize that your children may not even know what Watergate was.) The host, Ted Koppel, is a thinker. Somehow during the course of the thirty minutes on the air, Koppel and I got into the question of absolute values. We considered what was happening to America and how we were being immersed in the banality of television and losing our capacity to think.

When the show was over, Koppel said to me, "I would like to discuss these things with you. They are really interesting questions."

We drifted into the Green Room, where we sat down and chatted. Koppel said, "I don't understand you people, you new Religious Right people. I just don't understand you. You are intolerant."

"You come along," he said, "you have this set of values, and you want to cram them down my throat." He added, "People resent that, and that is why we are angry with you Christians."

"That just reflects our inability to explain to you what we believe," I replied.

I reminded him of a speech he gave at Duke University, a speech in which he said, "The Ten Commandments were Ten Commandments, not Ten Suggestions."

"Oh yes," he said, "but I mean something different." He talked about the Aristotelian view of the golden mean and how we live our lives aspiring to certain goals.

Then I tried to explain why we believe in absolutes—the root truth and what it means. I realized that I just was not getting through to this very intelligent man. For forty-five minutes I tried to explain my point of view. We don't want to cram our views down anybody's throat, I said. But we do want to be able to argue for our positions. Why can't I do that without being called a bigot?

Koppel believed, as many others do today, that once you confess a belief in moral absolutes, then you've claimed for your position a privilege that others don't enjoy.

The real underlying question is whether such a privilege exists—whether moral absolutes really exist.

Finally I tried one last example as a means of opening up the possibility that moral absolutes really exist. "Ted," I asked, "you've been sailing, haven't you?"

"Yes, indeed."

"Have you ever gone sailing at night?"

He nodded.

"Well, how does one navigate at night?"

"Celestial navigation. You take shots at the stars." And he started explaining celestial navigation.

"What would happen to your sailing at night," I asked, "if the stars were always in a random, different position? You can navigate only because you know where the stars are—at all times."

"Ah." He nodded. "I see. I see your point."

"The stars are out there," I said, "and they are in a fixed position. There is an order to the universe. If there is an order to the universe, there is a moral order by which we live. Civilization in the beginning of time—not just Bible-believing Christians but civilization in the beginning of time—believed that there is a moral order by which we live. It is a fixed moral order with absolutes, but no one can make you live by it. If you are sailing at night and you don't want to look at those stars, no one can make you look at them. But whether you look at them or not, they are there."

This sailing analogy might help you explain the nature of moral absolutes and show the importance of giving a reasoned response to accusations of intolerance.

Q 54: *Why is Christianity oppressive to women?*

Many young people today are concerned about the rights and roles of women in society. How could they not be, given all the attention that society has given to this subject, both for good and for ill, in recent years?

Those who argue that Christianity is oppressive to women are the ones on whom the burden of proof rests. A simple comparison of the "Christian" West with, say, the Islamic world shows a vast difference in the way society thinks about women. Who will doubt that that part of the world most influenced over the centuries by the gospel of Jesus Christ holds out more opportunity and more freedom for women than the Islamic nations do?

The fact is, Jesus was the great liberator of women. No other person in human history has done as much to make it possible for women to realize their full potential as image bearers of God. He spoke directly to women in public at a time when this was not acceptable, a time when much of the world considered women to be little more than personal possessions. (The "enlightened" Romans had so little regard for women that they often exposed infant girls to death by wild beasts or simply threw them in the Tiber River.) Jesus' relationship with women was one of tenderness, caring, and concern; he treated them with absolute equal dignity. John 4 presents an incredible account of Jesus' presenting the gospel to a scorned woman who had had five different husbands and was then living in adultery. John 4:39 indicates that the woman's own testimony brought many other townspeople to Christ. And at Jesus' resurrection he chose to show himself to women who had come to mourn his death.

The apostles Paul and Peter continued this honoring of women as equal-with-men image bearers of God. Paul indicates that we are all equal in Christ, all loved by God and called to serve him (Gal. 3:28-29). Though some female activists and others take offense at the biblical mandate that wives are to be in submission to their husbands, they fail to look at the corresponding and even greater demand placed on husbands. Husbands are commanded to love their wives as Christ loved the church, honoring them as they would their own bodies and being willing to sacrifice everything for their well-being (Eph. 5:25-33). This means that a husband must be willing to give his life for his wife. Peter, likewise, commanded husbands to regard their wives with understanding and care (1 Pet. 3:7). In the churches led by Peter and Paul, women taught other women and assisted their husbands in training others for the work of the Lord (Acts 18:26). Many of the people whom Paul saluted as coworkers in the work of the Lord were women (see, for example, Romans 16).

Throughout the centuries the church has continued this tradition. Yes, there has been some abuse of women—even in the name of Christ—but time and again people grounded in the Christian worldview have valued women and their roles.

Here are a few examples: Writing a history of England, the Venerable Bede said of seventh-century Abbess Hilda of Whitby: "So great was her prudence that not only ordinary folk, but kings and princes used to come and ask her advice in their difficulties." Clare of Assisi worked alongside Saint Francis. Saint Bridget of Sweden counseled kings, queens, and popes of her day. Saint Jane Frances de Chantal labored with Bishop Francis de Sales. And Hannah More, a devout Christian, was a key player along with William Wilberforce in the Clapham Sect in British reforms that included the end of the slave trade.

On this side of the Atlantic, Christian women played a crucial role in the abolition campaign. Among the better-known names were Quaker minister Lucretia Mott and an African-American named Sojourner Truth. In the fight for a woman's right to vote, no name is more prominent than that of another devout Quaker, Susan B. Anthony. Many other Christian women, including Anna Howard Shaw, Alice Paul, and Laura Clay, also fought for their right to vote.

People who complain that Christianity is oppressive to women do not understand either the Scriptures or the record of history.

Q 55: *How can Christians condemn homosexuals for being the way God made them?*

First, we need to understand that Christian thinking about such questions begins and ends with the fact of God's love. What does a loving God want for homosexuals? Did he make them the way they are, or is their sexual preference a *consequence* of what makes our world a broken one?

Many "secular sermons" would attempt to convince us that homosexuality is genetically determined, but they fly in the face of empirical evidence to the contrary. Researchers looking for a gay gene periodically announce new evidence of its existence, but the evidence quickly evaporates when other researchers examine it. For example, a National Institutes of Health study, authored by Dean Hamer, reported the alleged existence of a genetic marker that predisposes individuals to homosexual behaviors.

In a review of Hamer's research, however, geneticist Dr. Evan Balaban said that Hamer's research was seriously flawed in both its methodology and its basic assumptions—not surprising, perhaps, given that Hamer himself is a homosexual activist whose agenda may have biased the results of his research. Most telling of all is the fact that many of the gay men in Hamer's study did *not* have the genetic marker that he says is linked to homosexual behavior.

If homosexuality is not genetically determined, then to some degree the behavior involves an element of choice. That doesn't mean that some people don't have a predisposition to homosexuality—they do, just as straight people have predispositions they must control.

David Persing, a molecular genetics researcher and a Christian, says that the biblical teaching that all of nature is fallen includes our genetic heritage. As a result, we *all* have inborn tendencies toward various forms of sinful behaviors, from alcoholism to heterosexual addiction to homosexuality. But this fact does not excuse the choice to sin, Persing says. Christianity calls all of us to struggle against our natural tendencies. Whatever those inclinations are, we still have room for making real moral choices.

As Christians we need to stand against the philosophy of genetic determinism, which reduces people—such as Alan Medinger—to pawns.

Alan was a practicing homosexual for seventeen years. Today he is a Christian and the founder of Regeneration, a ministry to homosexuals. "Homosexuality isn't just about sexual relations," Medinger says. "It's a complete personality orientation, a set of attitudes toward masculinity and femininity."

Medinger attributes homosexuality to an interruption in the normal process of maturing—often due to emotional trauma or abuse. And in *The Other Way Out,* the Reverend Paul Brenton notes that many men's struggles with homosexuality have their roots in molestation or emotional abuse. They have twisted images of themselves as being less than real men, Brenton says. "Many of them feel trapped in their life-style and genuinely want to get out."

That was certainly the case for John Paulk, formerly a male prostitute and female impersonator. His life as a homosexual was a misguided and painful attempt to deal with the emotional pain of rejection. In *Every Student's Choice* he writes, "In my past there were many masks I hid behind to protect myself."

John is now married to Anne, a former lesbian with a similar story. It was her underlying need for love and acceptance that drove her into lesbianism, she says, until Christian friends reached out to her with genuine friendship.

John and Anne are quick to talk about the transforming power of God in their lives. The good news of Christ's love brought them out of homosexuality. "The Lord's transforming power was so evident during our wedding," John said later, "that my mother and stepfather prayed to receive the Lord that night."

That's a powerful testimony, and it demonstrates a powerful truth: The gospel *can* free homosexuals to live in monogamous heterosexual relationships. Of course, gaining freedom from homosexuality often involves a long, difficult road that retraces the process of development in order to create a heterosexual identity. The point is that homosexuals can find freedom and healing.

A follow-up question might be: Why should homosexuals seek this freedom? Does the evidence suggest that there are practical reasons for the biblical position?

The gay lifestyle exacts a heavy personal cost. According to Bob Davies, executive director of Exodus International, a ministry to homosexuals, 25 to 33 percent of homosexuals are alcoholics, compared with 7 percent of the general population. And homosexual men are six times more likely than straight men to attempt suicide. (Gay advocates insist that these statistics reflect society's prejudice against homosexuals.)

Time and time again, scientists have claimed that particular genes or chromosomal regions are associated with behavioral traits, only to withdraw their findings when they were not replicated. . . . All were announced with great fanfare; all were greeted unskeptically in the popular press; all are now in disrepute.

C. Mann, "Genes and Behavior"

The statistics tell a brighter story for those who are able to come to grips with the emotional and physical abuse they have suffered. According to Bill Consiglio, director of Hope Ministries, 40 percent of homosexuals who seek change "move into full heterosexuality, with many entering marriage and parenthood." An additional 40 percent are able to commit themselves to living as celibate Christian singles.

Others sources agree. Therapy directed toward a change in sexual preference often works. For example, a 1974 Masters and Johnson study found that therapy had a success rate of more than 70 percent after a six-year follow-up. And in 1986 a Dutch psychoanalyst studied 101 patients and found a 65 percent success rate.

But today society is blocking the potential for healing—ironically by becoming too accepting of the gay lifestyle. As one former lesbian puts it, pro-gay groups are actually making it hard for those who want to break out of their destructive lifestyle to do so. Since, in their minds, there's "nothing wrong" with being gay, homosexuals should have no desire to be healed.

Given that the gay lifestyle brings suffering and often tragedy, what's the compassionate response? Anne Paulk says, "As a lesbian I found hurt people just [looking for] love. As a Christian I found loving people just wanting to heal my hurt." As Christians, we cannot deny the Bible's teaching that homosexuality is a sin (Rom. 1:24-27), yet we stand with homosexuals, helping them fight this destructive sin in their lives. Just as we pray they will stand with us in our struggles.

Q 56: How can anyone defend Christianity when religion has been responsible for so many wars and other atrocities? What about the Crusades and the Spanish Inquisition?

I've heard this question many times—we all have. In a *New York Times* article, historian Arthur Schlesinger went so far as to say that a belief in absolute truth is responsible for war, slavery, persecution, and torture. This objection kept famous writer and eventual convert Malcolm Muggeridge from the faith for years.

Recently I was talking to a friend who is not a believer, and he brought up the same matter. "Chuck," he said, "everything you say about Christianity sounds good. But what bothers me is the historical record. The Crusades, the Inquisition—all the terrible things done in the name of Christ."

"True," I said. "But just remember, that's nothing compared to the things done in the name of secular faiths. Think of Hitler—six million Jews murdered in the Holocaust. And Stalin—some fifty million people slaughtered in the Gulag. The fruits of atheism are much, much worse than any abuse of Christianity.

"Take a simple body count," I said. "The Christian record includes the Crusades and the Inquisition. But the crusading armies were tiny by modern standards, and medieval warfare consisted mostly of isolated battles between professional soldiers.

"Contrast that to what happened in World War II, when the Nazis plunged the whole world into war—and exterminated millions of people in concentration camps.

"By modern standards the Inquisition was small potatoes, too. It's estimated that three thousand people were killed over a period of three hundred years. That's three thousand too many, of course, but compare it with the sixty million killed during seventy years of communist oppression."

I went on to explain that when a Hitler or a Stalin commits atrocities, he is acting out his ideology. He's revealing the logical consequences of what he believes. When Christians are cruel, they are acting *contrary* to what they believe.

But when Christians act in accord with their faith, even in small measure, the result is a goodness that the world knows nothing about. Around the world Christians have built schools, universities, orphanages, and hospitals. They have supported law and public morality. They have rescued children thrown out to die. They have helped the poor and visited those in prison.

The evidence from history is clear: Despite our human faults, Christianity has made the world and the people in it far better than they would have been without it.

Q 57: *Why are Christians anti-intellectual?*

In the magazine *Free Inquiry,* British biologist Richard Dawkins calls religion a mental virus—a false belief that infects your mind the way a virus infects your body. Consider the symptoms, Dawkins writes. People don't adopt a religion after carefully weighing the evidence; faith is "caught" the way a cold is. It spreads from person to person like an infection, especially in families. For those who convert, Dawkins says, an evangelist may be the infectious agent. Revivals are virtual epidemics of faith.

Well, it's a clever biological metaphor, but I say that Dr. Dawkins is a bit too quick with his diagnosis, as are others who accuse Christians of being irrational. While it's true that many of us learn our religious faith at our parents' knees, the way we learn about religion is a separate question from whether or not what we learned is true.

No matter what any of us learned as children, we all come to a point when we make our own commitments—when we believe because we are personally convinced by experience and evidence. Unlike some religions, Christianity does not preach a mystical experience that overrides reason. Instead, Scripture connects its message to historical events that could be seen and confirmed by anyone present at the time they occurred—from Elijah's calling down fire from heaven on Mount Carmel to Jesus' public crucifixion and resurrection from the dead.

When Dawkins calls religion a virus, he's ignoring the real character of Christianity. He's assuming that people accept it without any intelligent reasons—that their acceptance of it is driven by sheer emotional need.

We've heard other versions of this same sentiment before. It's nothing but the old argument that religion is a crutch for weak people. Karl Marx called religion the "opiate of the people." Sigmund Freud labeled it a neurosis.

But notice that Dawkins and Marx and Freud never proved that religion is a mental sickness. They simply assumed that Christianity was false and then set out to identify some aberration of the mind to explain why people still believe it. The entire argument is hopelessly circular. First it assumes that Christianity is false; then it diagnoses faith as a sickness in order to convince people that it's false.

Genuine Christian faith doesn't infect your mind; it respects your mind. Christians ought to be the most tough-minded people of all. If truth is truth, then any honest question should not be a threat to us. We don't need to back away from the hard questions. In fact, because Christ is the embodiment of truth, we as Christians have the greatest freedom to ask the hard questions ourselves, and we should not feel threatened when other people ask those questions of us. For this reason no honest search for truth can be against the Christian faith.

Indeed, great Christians down through the ages have demonstrated that Christianity is anything but anti-intellectual. Believers, driven by their Christian faith, have produced some of the greatest treasures of art and made some of the greatest scientific advances in the history of the West.

A case in point, one that the secular world is reluctant to acknowledge, is Dutch artist Vincent van Gogh. His life is the subject of a highly acclaimed French film. But you'll never learn what van Gogh was really like from this movie. It omits a central fact of van Gogh's life: his deep Christian faith.

As a young man, van Gogh wanted to become a pastor. But his hopes were dashed when he flunked out of seminary. Undaunted, he preached the gospel to destitute coal miners, living among them and sharing their poverty. Van Gogh's goal was thwarted once again when he began to show signs of mental instability and lost the financial support of his mission society.

It was then that he turned to art, producing hundreds of great paintings. He continued to battle with mental illness until age thirty-seven when, suffering from delusions that compromised his judgment, he committed suicide.

It's a tragic story. But almost equally tragic is the fact that we almost never hear about it. Books on art history usually suppress the full story, carefully scrubbing out any reference to van Gogh's strong Christian faith.

And van Gogh's story isn't the only one. Many people know the name of the great painter Rembrandt, but they don't know that he, too, was a devout Christian. Poet Samuel Coleridge became an icon of the drug culture in the 1960s because he composed many of his poems under the influence of opium. But no one mentions the fact that Coleridge found freedom from his opium addiction by turning to Jesus Christ.

Most people know that composers Bach and Handel were Christians. But what about Vivaldi? Vivaldi was a man of the cloth, nicknamed the Red Priest for his bright red hair. Antonín Dvořák, with his lively Slavic melodies, was a sturdy Christian believer. Felix Mendelssohn, the son of Jewish parents, was a devout Lutheran.

The notebooks of scientists Copernicus, Kepler, Newton, and Pascal overflow with praise to the Creator.

Throughout history many of the greatest masters of the English language have been Christian poets. Think of John Donne, who wrote such memorable lines as "Death be not proud"; "No man is an island"; and "Never send to know for whom the bell tolls; it tolls for thee."

Think of John Milton, who composed the epic poem *Paradise Lost* to "justify the ways of God to men." And the rich language of poet Gerard Manley Hopkins is incomparable: "The world is charged with the grandeur of God. It will flame out, like shining from shook foil."

Christians have made major contributions in virtually every field of art and scholarship. Yet modern history books rarely mention the role faith has played in building our culture. That makes it easy for non-Christians to belittle Christians as bumbling know-nothings. And Christians have been cut off from understanding the rich cultural and intellectual heritage that is rightfully ours.

Q 58: *Why don't Christians care more about ecology?*

For years New Agers have blamed the ecological crisis on Christianity. But the Bible actually teaches a very high view of creation. When God put Adam in the Garden, he instructed him to till it and keep it. The Hebrew words for those tasks mean "to serve" and "to take care of." Genesis teaches that humans have "dominion" over nature, but that doesn't mean arbitrary rule; it means stewardship. This is God's world, and we're accountable to him for the way we treat it.

Granted, Westerners have often abused nature. But that didn't stem from Christianity; it came from humanism. As Western culture rejected the Bible, it no longer regarded humanity as God's servants but as the pinnacle of evolution, the victor in the Darwinian struggle for existence, the victor who owes nothing to anyone.

Think back to the nineteenth century: The robber barons of industry didn't appeal to Christianity to justify their cutthroat tactics. They appealed to evolution. Listen to the words of William Graham Sumner, America's most influential social Darwinist: "There can be no rights against Nature," he wrote, "except to get out of her whatever we can."

Today we are appalled at such a crass attitude, and rightly so. But the antidote to Western humanism is not Eastern pantheism, what has been called "nature-based religion." Pantheism—the belief that everything partakes of Deity, everything is God—denies that humans are unique; it puts us on the same level as the trees and the grass.

> *The value of the things is not in themselves autonomously, but that God made them— and thus they deserve to be treated with high respect. . . . When you are driving an ax into the tree when you need firewood, you are not cutting down a person; you are cutting a tree. . . . We must realize that God made [the tree] and it deserves respect because He made it* **as a tree.**
>
> Francis Schaeffer, *Pollution and the Death of Man*

But humans do have unique powers that no other organisms have. The only religion that can solve our ecological problems is one that acknowledges our uniqueness and then gives ethical guidelines that direct our unique capabilities. Christianity does just that: It teaches that God made humans in his image to be stewards over his creation.

KEY POINTS IN BRIEF

✓ Because God made the universe and humankind, both the world and human beings have an objective reality. It is this objective reality that is the basis for the biblical standards of right and wrong.

✓ Everyone's emotions are real enough *as emotions*. But we need to base our ethical decisions on truth—objective reality—rather than on what we "feel" is right.

✓ Christians believe in absolutes, but that does not mean they embrace absolutism, a rigid mentality that is inflexible, irrational, and hostile. Christians must express their belief in absolutes in a caring, winning way.

✓ Studies have shown that Christians are actually more tolerant than their secular neighbors. They are also far more deeply concerned about the poor and disenfranchised.

✓ The true meaning of tolerance is based on judgment; it's respecting the rights of others to hold their opinions even when we believe those opinions are wrong.

✓ Jesus Christ clearly demonstrated that men and women are equal in God's eyes. Christianity, for the most part, has been the great liberator of women, as we can see when we contrast Western culture and other world cultures.

✓ Christianity calls homosexuals to recover from their sexual inclinations, just as it calls heterosexuals to abstain from promiscuity and other vices. Homosexuality is wrong, and there are good practical reasons for homosexuals to seek help with their sexual disposition.

✓ Although such historical sins as the Crusades and the Inquisition are serious blights on the Christian record, far more killing and destruction have been visited on humankind in the name of secular ideologies than in the name of Christ.

✓ Far from being anti-intellectual, the Christian faith gives the believer every confidence that "all truth is God's truth." Most of the glories of Western civilization in science, the arts, and the humanities have been the result of Christians' inquiries into the nature of the world God made.

CHAPTER 8

Why Shouldn't I . . . ?
Sex, Love, and Marriage

Q 59: *Don't all the negative rules Christians have about sex come from a hatred for the body? Don't they treat the body as if it were dirty?*

The tendency to view the human body as unclean arises from the belief that we can split the mind and body; this is called *dualism*. This error has afflicted not only Christianity but also many other ways of thinking in every culture and time.

We saw a horrible instance of this in the tragic Heaven's Gate cult. The cult members were easy to recognize. Every time they left their Rancho Santa Fe mansion, they looked exactly alike: they all sported black clothing, Nike sneakers, and buzz-cut hair. When police entered the mansion and found the bodies, they first thought that all thirty-nine cult members were young men.

One of the most puzzling aspects of this strange cult was their obsessive conformity. But the explanation is actually simple. The Heaven's Gate cult taught a philosophy that is based in a hatred of all things physical—especially the physical body.

The cult members believed that to achieve salvation they had to shed their earthly bodies. They viewed the body as a sort of prison that has entrapped the soul, and they believed that salvation would occur when the soul left the body. That's why they referred to their bodies as "vehicles" or "containers." (Interestingly this is the principle used to justify promiscuity: Treat the body as if it were distinct from the self—a lie that serves both bestial and falsely transcendent purposes.) The cult prohibited marriage and all sexual activity and tried to avoid what they called "all human-mammalian behavior."

Like the Heaven's Gate members, all dualists believe not only in the existence of a radical split between the body and the soul but also that the human body and material world are evil.

Dualism had a particularly damaging influence on the Christian church in its early centuries. But it was rightly denounced as a heresy because Scripture explicitly rejects dualism. Genesis teaches that God created the heavens and the earth, including the human body. God said that he was pleased with his creation. The apostle Paul refers to our body as the temple of the Holy Spirit and writes to Timothy, "Everything God created is good" (1 Tim. 4:4).

As Paul Tillich writes, this is the meaning of the first article of the Apostles' Creed: "I believe in God the Father Almighty, maker of heaven and earth." By this confession, Christianity separated itself from the dualism that was inherent in paganism. In the Christian understanding, body, mind, and soul are one. It is the modern secularist who demeans the human body, demanding control over it and considering it something to be used for one's pleasure.

The biblical message is clear: The human body itself is not evil; it's the *desires* of the flesh—things like fornication, jealousy, and drunkenness—that are sinful and must be brought under control.

That's why it's so important to grasp the full message of the biblical worldview. Christianity's appreciation for the goodness of creation leads us to *value* that creation, including the body; we are meant to care for the body by not violating its moral order. Christianity's prohibitions against premarital sex, homosexuality, and other forms of sexual license are not repressive rules meant to deny us pleasure. They are there to respect human dignity and to enable the Christian's freedom in the true pleasures of being God's creatures.

Q 60: *Why are Christians so hung up about sex?*

Many people besides our teenagers believe that it's not healthy to repress our feelings, that we would all be better off if sex became just one of life's great pleasures. President Clinton's AIDS policy coordinator once called America a repressed Victorian society. The very idea of teaching kids to say no to sex, Kristine Gebbie said, is "criminal." It "spreads fear," robbing children of a positive view of sexuality. What we really ought to teach kids, Gebbie went on, is that sex is "an essentially pleasurable and important thing."

In the America I know, we're so repressed that people like Madonna can make a fortune from sexual posturing. So Victorian that every other commercial uses sexual innuendo to sell products. So puritanical that *Playboy* and *Hustler* are sold at neighborhood 7-Eleven stores.

I think we can safely say that people already know sexuality is a "pleasurable thing." What they desperately need to learn is that sex can actually be much *more* satisfying when kept within the bounds of biblical morality.

Statistics indicate that modern-day "Victorians"—the name some people give to conservative Christians—actually enjoy the most satisfying sex lives. Several years ago *Redbook* magazine ran a reader survey and found, to its own surprise, that women who characterized themselves as "strongly religious" reported greater sexual satisfaction than the nonreligious survey respondents.

In fact, at the same time Ms. Gebbie was delivering her blasts against conservative sexual morality, the Southern Baptists were holding a fall festival entitled "Celebrating Sex in Your Marriage." Richard Land, spokesperson for the denomination, commented that Ms. Gebbie seems to be equating abstinence *outside* marriage with a low view of sex *within* marriage.

But the biblical ethic does not teach a low view of sex. If Ms. Gebbie would take a closer look at the Book that shapes the attitudes of those supposedly Victorian Christians, she would find the most positive sex-education program ever designed. Far from repressing sexuality, the Bible celebrates it. The Song of Solomon is a tender picture of the desire a husband and wife feel for one another.

The New Testament takes this attitude even further, with Paul teaching in 1 Corinthians 7 that husbands and wives should not deprive one another of sexual relations—that sexuality is an important part of the marriage relationship.

Imagine that: The Bible actually orders married couples not to deny their sexual desires.

Q 61: *Why should I wait to have sex until I'm married?*

Once again, the Bible's teaching on sexuality and marriage centers on who God made us to be—the type of creatures we are. We are not just a mind that resides in a body. We don't use our body like a conveyance or tool for particular purposes. Mind and body compose a unity: They are one. Any sexual act represents a giving of the person—the whole person—to another. That's why the Bible speaks of marriage as two people becoming "one flesh." That's what happens literally, and the union of our bodies has a psychological and spiritual dimension whether or not we like it.

Scripture is also clear about the impact of sexual sin: "Run away from sexual sin! No other sin so clearly affects the body as this one does. For sexual immorality is a sin against your own body" (1 Cor. 6:18, NLT).

As Princeton professor Robert George said in "Why Integrity Matters," a speech given at the National Prayer Breakfast, "Where sex is sought purely for pleasure, or as a means of inducing feelings of emotional closeness, or for some other extrinsic [impersonal] end, the body is reduced to the status of sub-personal, purely instrumental, reality. This existential separation of the body and the conscious and the experiential part of the self serves literally to *dis*-integrate the person. It takes the person apart, so the good of having it all together—being a dynamically unified actor, body, mind, and spirit in harmony—is destroyed."

In other words, the promiscuous person pledges himself or herself to love the other person through the act of sexual intercourse but then denies this same commitment mentally. The break that comes between the meaning of the action and the person's own feeling about it inevitably creates emotional and spiritual suffering. The person lives a lie. He or she may lose the ability to distinguish real emotions from their counterfeits; the person may, in fact, damage or destroy his or her ability to love.

This may seem extreme, but how else would one account for our eroticized culture and the popular complaint of both sexes that love is impossible to find?

> ### *Real love . . . can stand the test of time without physical intimacy. The sexually active lose objectivity.*
>
> Michael McManus, *Marriage Savers*

I was watching a wonderful old movie the other day, *Yours, Mine, and Ours.* The lead character (played by Henry Fonda) is taking his pregnant wife (played by Lucille Ball) to the hospital to have a baby. On the way there they stumble on their teenage daughter and her pawing boyfriend. The girl is fending off the boy's advances but wondering exactly why. She says her boyfriend insists that she would sleep with him if she loved him.

Fonda points out that real love and real sex is about what he's trying to do—get his wife to the hospital to usher new life into the world. "This is what it's all about," Fonda says. "If you want to know what love really is, take a good look around you. Take a good look at your mother."

Lucille Ball interjects, "Not now."

"Yes now," Fonda says. "Till you're ready for it all, the rest is just a big fraud. . . . Life isn't a love-in. It's the dishes and the shoe repairman and ground round instead of roast beef."

His daughter tries to counter her father, "But Larry [her boyfriend] said—"

Fonda interrupts. "I'll tell you something else. It isn't going to bed with a man that proves you're in love with him. It's getting up in the morning facing the drab, miserable, wonderful, everyday world with him that counts."

Q 62: *But everybody takes having sex before marriage for granted.*
How can our whole society be wrong?

Sadly, this teenage observation is dead right. Sex outside of marriage is the norm in almost every sitcom, movie, and love song. For a teenager to resist people's common expectations becomes a heroic and profoundly countercultural act.

But some young people are responding to this challenge. "Everyone" doesn't go along with the mass media message.

A recent issue of *American Demographics* magazine introduced readers to Ryan K., a nineteen-year-old student at Georgetown University. While Ryan is in many respects like the kids you see depicted on the screen—right down to a pierced eyebrow—his attitudes toward sex and morality are remarkably traditional.

> *No man or woman, boy or girl, should put their trust in a piece of rubber. A condom never stopped a person from experiencing a broken heart or a shattered dream no matter how many you put on. For singles—SAFE SEX IS NO SEX. Period. That's a 100 percent guarantee.*
>
> A. C. Green, L.A. Lakers

Ryan says he has no intention of living with a woman outside of marriage. He told *American Demographics* that he plans to have sex with his future bride for the first time on their wedding night.

And Ryan isn't alone in his embrace of more traditional sexual mores. In the past two decades the number of eighteen- to twenty-four-year-olds who say "it's always wrong to have sex before marriage" has doubled. In the past two years, the percentage of unmarried couples who live together has dropped by nearly a third—a staggering reversal of past trends.

Kirsty Doig, vice president of a market research group called Youth Intelligence, says these figures indicate a major new trend among the young—a trend she labels "neotraditionalism." Other experts agree, predicting a surge in teen marriages and larger families.

What's even more fascinating than these trends are the reasons behind them. Doig told *American Demographics* that today's eighteen- to twenty-four-year-olds "have not had a lot of stability in their lives." As a result we're seeing "a backlash, a return to tradition and ritual. And that includes marriage."

This openness to tradition presents Christians with an incredible opportunity for witness. We know that as positive as these trends are, they are not enough. These kids are doing the right thing. Now they need to embrace the right reasons for doing these things.

By teaching your teenager about God's purposes in creating sexuality, you can help him or her find the true fulfillment of sexuality in marriage and family. You can inspire a different set of expectations that will give your teenager a reason for rejecting common and totally misleading assumptions about premarital sex.

Q 63: *But a guy needs sex. Isn't it just a natural function?*

According to the *New York Times,* the city's pools were the site of a fad called "the whirlpool." Twenty to thirty boys would link arms in a circle and surround a solitary girl. The boys would close in on her, dunk her head under the water, tear off her bathing suit, and grab at her. The problem grew so severe that several teenage boys were arrested for sexual assault.

Reporters asked several teens how they accounted for the boys' predatory behavior. "It's nature," one boy replied. "Look at a female dog and a male dog. It's the same thing: You see twenty male dogs on a female dog. It's the male nature, in a way."

How utterly repugnant. But how utterly consistent with what these kids are being taught not only in schools but also in popular culture.

The great prophet of sex education was Alfred Kinsey, who built his theory of sexuality squarely on the foundation of scientific naturalism. Kinsey taught that humans are part of nature—nothing more. As a result, he evaluated every form of sexual activity in terms of its role in the lives of the lower species. Any behavior found among the lower animals Kinsey regarded as natural for humans as well.

In his words, it is "part of the normal mammalian picture."

Kinsey—as we've seen with others—was working on the assumption of evolution. Evolution teaches an unbroken continuity between humans and the animal world. And if we are simply advanced animals, then our guide to behavior is whatever the animals do. As Kinsey puts it, in sexual matters humans should follow the example of "our mammalian forebears."

Kinsey's philosophy has been the authority among sex educators ever since the 1950s. And it sounds to me as if some New York boys have grasped it precisely. "Look at a female dog and a male dog" is merely a vernacular translation of Kinsey's more sophisticated talk about "the normal mammalian picture."

The Bible does not teach that we are merely dogs in heat. It teaches that we are bearers of the image of God. We are indeed creatures, but we have been made only a little lower than the angels (Ps. 8:5). We do not act just out of instinct. We choose not only how we act but also the basis on which we act.

Sex is not merely a natural function. It's a profound expression, as we've said before, of body, mind, and spirit. The Bible says that through sexual intercourse a man and a woman become "one flesh," meaning not merely that the two are joined physically but that through this physical union they pledge themselves to love one another. Sex without love is always a lie, because the sexual act contains an inherent meaning—an implicit promise—to love the other person. This meaning is not dependent on how we choose to think about what we are doing; it belongs to the act itself. And that's why so much ill-feeling is generated by casual sex. One person or both people feel lied to, even if both people try to convince themselves they are only engaging in a pleasurable activity.

Over time promiscuous behavior can actually convince a person that sexuality exists only for our pleasure—just as over time any lie or rationalization becomes increasingly convincing. But promiscuity actually alienates the person from true emotion; the person is no longer able to understand the full meaning of sexual union. This is why the Bible teaches that fornication and adultery are sins against ourselves—they are lies we are telling ourselves. They are lies that have disastrous consequences in our emotional and spiritual lives.

Q 64: *Why has date rape become such a problem?*

The answer is in the old biblical principle: You reap what you sow. For years, our society has sown the seed of sexual permissiveness. Sex dominates movies, television, and popular music. As we'll discuss in a later education chapter, in some places a young man is handed a package of condoms in high school. A clear signal—from school authorities no less—that he's expected to be sexually active.

The old code of chivalry has been discredited. Remember the time when no man could claim to be civilized unless he showed courtesy and protectiveness toward women?

Now some men have adopted a new code in its place: that a real man takes whatever he can get sexually, that a real man doesn't take no for an answer.

The loss of the older code puts women at risk. To state the obvious, there are biological differences between the sexes. It's easier to assault a woman than a man. When moral and social constraints are lifted, it's women who become more vulnerable.

Feminists say the solution to date rape is for men to respect women who say no. Certainly men should, but that's not enough; after all, they shouldn't be asking the question in the first place. (That assumes that date rape happens after a discussion. Most date rape is a violent, forcible act that does not even stop to take into account that another person is involved, let alone that the person has a belief system that says, "No! I don't want to do this.") The real problem is that sex has been stripped of its moral dimension. It's been reduced to a clash of personal desires.

The man says "I want" and the woman says "I don't want," but they have no moral principles to support their inclinations, no code of decency common to both sexes and to the larger society. It's one private will pitted against the other. Add alcohol or drugs to the equation, and you have a classic setup for date rape.

These violent acts have a devastating effect in women's lives, interfering with their ability to mature and cope with other stresses in life, and affecting the health and well-being of their future families. Make no mistake: Date rape is rape, with all of rape's accompanying trauma.

America needs a recommitment to the idea that sex is more than a private choice. It's a moral issue. There are moral standards transcending what you or I may want at the moment—not only in sex but in every area of life.

The best way of convincing young men to treat women with respect is to educate them in the traditional virtues, which make it a disgrace to treat anyone basely, dishonestly, or exploitatively.

Waller R. Newell, "The Crisis of Manliness"

The 1960s sowed the slogans of free sex. Today we are reaping a harvest of forced sex. In sex as in politics, freedom without moral restraints leads to might making right—or brutally disregarding a person's protests.

Parents of teenage sons should be especially careful to inculcate respect for young women as people. In some cases, young men may have to act on what they know to be true about their dates—that they are persons made in the image of God—even when the young women they are with, influenced by our culture, are ready to trade sex for affection. Our sons need to understand that there can be no compromises on this issue.

Parents of teenage daughters should help them understand that they need to speak out when a young man crosses a line sexually. Strengthen your daughter's ability to stand up to young men by listening to her and letting her know that you respect and value her opinions. Teach her that she is an image bearer of God and because she is, she has a right and responsibility to protect that image in her body and to expect others to respect that right as well.

Q 65: *Shouldn't people be free to end a marriage when it's no longer fulfilling?*

In this instance I would like to ask a question in turn. What would you have said to a friend of mine who recently walked into my office and told me that his wife of eleven years had announced that she wanted to separate? In a matter of a few moments, his life and his little boy's life were turned upside down. He didn't want his wife to leave him, but he had no recourse and no legal or other social remedy other than simply letting her go.

Unfortunately my friend's tragic story is not unusual. Every day thousands of husbands and wives receive the same bad news. No-fault divorce laws give people legal encouragement to treat their marriage vows like pie crust—easily made, easily broken.

As Maggie Gallagher writes in her book *The Abolition of Marriage,* for thirty years no-fault divorce laws have taught the American people that marriage is merely a temporary arrangement—one that can be dissolved at the whim of either party.

But fortunately "pie-crust" marriage vows may soon become a thing of the past, at least in some states. Louisiana, along with several other states, has passed a law called the Covenant Marriage Act as an option for couples committed to the sanctity of marriage.

Louisiana couples may now choose between a marriage license that permits a "no-fault" divorce and a license for a "covenant marriage"—one that commits them to marriage for life. In covenant marriage, the law will recognize adultery, abuse, or abandonment (or a lengthy separation) as the only legal grounds for divorce. If a couple chooses covenant marriage, they're required to have premarital counseling.

But if the couple decides *against* a covenant marriage—well, at least both bride and groom will know that their intended spouse plans to walk down the aisle with his or her fingers crossed.

This is important information for potential spouses to know because some 80 percent of divorces are unilateral, sought by just one spouse. As Maggie Gallagher writes in the journal *First Things,* a more accurate term for no-fault divorce would be "unilateral divorce on demand."

The Covenant Marriage Act now gives spouses some protection against unilateral divorce. Nobody is forced to choose covenant marriage, but if couples *do* choose it, the law requires that their commitment to spouse and children take precedence over personal desires for self-fulfillment.

> ## *Marriage is the bedrock upon which a family is built and upon which everyone in the family depends. The marriage is "where it's at" and always will be.*
>
> John Rosemond, "Because I Said So"

The new law is already making couples think twice about their wedding plans. Louisiana resident Mark McDonald told the *Washington Post,* "I told [my fiancée] that I didn't want to go through with it if she didn't want a [covenant marriage]. . . . I'm serious about making this a lifelong commitment."

And that is what marriage is about—a covenant between a man and a woman—for as long as they both shall live.

Jesus was very clear about his response to divorce. He specifically said that no person should separate what God has joined together (Matt. 19:6). The very purpose of a marriage is not "self" fulfillment but the fulfillment of the bond that unites two people. This is so much a part of the good for which men and women were created that Jesus chose to call himself the bridegroom and his church the bride. If there are problems in a marriage, then both spouses have a responsibility to work toward reconciliation.

Q 66: *Mom and Dad, since you divorced, I just can't respect you anymore. How can it be wrong for me to make my own decisions when you've made such bad ones?*

I want to be clear that teenagers of divorced parents must still honor their parents and obey them. They must honor their mother and father regardless of whether or not their parents have disobeyed God's laws. All parents have disobeyed in one way or another.

Many young people have understandable resentments in divorce situations, but they need to realize that resentments only make it more difficult to achieve a healthy, well-balanced life for themselves. Someone once said, "Resentments are like eating rat poison and expecting the rat to get sick." Teens must learn to forgive and to move beyond the pain, not only for their parents' sake but also for their own well-being.

It's also crucial that Christian parents model Christian parenthood even when the marriage relationship has been broken. If you are divorced, don't belittle your ex-spouse. Don't carry on financial or custodial negotiations through your children. Seek reconciliation on these issues. Go the extra mile to demonstrate love even in the midst of heartache. This will set an example your children will benefit from today and in the future.

Nothing is more important to your teenager than being able to grasp the biblical understanding of family—even in the midst of a marriage's failure—because if they don't get this straight, they are not likely to get much else straight in life. Many parents demonstrate heroic virtue in the midst of their difficult circumstances.

KEY POINTS IN BRIEF

✓ Christianity teaches that the body is the "temple of the Holy Spirit"—an entirely positive view toward physical life. The tendency to view the body as unclean comes from dualism, which results both in despising the body and also in using it promiscuously for illicit pleasure.

✓ The Bible teaches that sex is a good gift of God and that spouses should not withhold sex from each other.

✓ Because premarital sex is so widely accepted in the wider culture, sexual abstinence for teenagers is now a profoundly countercultural act. Parents should encourage and support their teens in every possible way as they respond to this challenge.

✓ The Bible's teaching on sexuality centers on who God made us to be—the type of creatures we are. Any sexual act represents a giving of the person—the whole person—to another. That's why the Bible speaks of marriage as two becoming "one flesh." This is why the Bible insists sexual relations are meant for married couples alone.

✓ Date rape and other violent acts against women are on the rise because the culture has taught us to regard ourselves as nothing more than animals. Christian parents need to teach their young sons to value women as persons—not sexual objects.

✓ Whether or not parents have followed the biblical teaching about divorce, their teenagers must still honor and obey them. Teenage children of divorce should look to Christ to take away their anger and resentments and give them the grace to forgive their parents.

CHAPTER 9

Should I Keep My Baby?
Life at the Limits: Pregnancy, Abortion, and Bioethics

Q 67: *What's the big deal about abortion? It's just a fetus, not a person.*

When it comes to abortion and "choice," we need to ask an underlying question: What are we choosing?

The practice of abortion depends on dehumanizing the fetus—believing that it's just a pile of cells, just fetal matter.

For centuries the process of a child's growth in a mother's womb was shrouded in mystery. But today's medical technology has opened a window to the womb. Using reflected sound waves, ultrasound produces a moving picture of the baby wiggling and waving its arms inside the mother's uterus.

Ultrasound has revealed that babies in the womb are much more aware of the outside world than anyone had previously imagined. A bright light placed near the mother's abdomen startles the baby and causes it to turn away. But the baby is attracted to a soft light and turns toward it. A loud buzzer will make the baby jump. But the baby responds to the sound of a soft rattle by taking its thumb out of its mouth and looking in the direction of the sound. A baby in the womb even comes to recognize its mother's voice.

Ultrasound makes a fetus seem more human. In fact, the word *fetus* no longer seems fitting once you've seen how that little person moves and responds. "Fetus" sounds too technical, too abstract. We instinctively use the word *baby*.

Medical technology has verified what the psalmist had already told us long ago: "You made all the delicate, inner parts of my body and knit me together in my mother's womb. . . . You watched me as I was being formed in utter seclusion, as I was woven together in the dark of the womb. You saw me before I was born" (Ps. 139:13-16, NLT).

What would happen if every woman considering an abortion saw an ultrasound of her baby beforehand?

Let me tell you a true story. A young woman—I'll call her Brenda—discovered that she was pregnant. It was an unplanned pregnancy, and when Brenda announced it at the office, she was noticeably glum.

But a few weeks later Brenda came bouncing into the office full of excitement. In her hand were ultrasound photos. Proudly she passed the photos around among her coworkers. "Do you want to see my baby?" she asked. "Look how big she is."

Seeing her baby on ultrasound helped Brenda begin bonding with her baby even before birth.

Another story illustrates the terrible cost of abortion—of how much is lost when we take the life of a preborn child.

It's the 1930s, when out-of-wedlock pregnancy is rare and shocking. A fourteen-year-old girl, the daughter of a clergyman, finds herself pregnant. What should she do?

Today a frightened teenager would likely abort her child. But sixty years ago abortion was illegal, and the story of that fourteen-year-old helps us understand the true cost of abortion.

The wonderfully moving book *A Severe Mercy* by the late Sheldon Vanauken tells the story of the spiritual pilgrimage the author shared with his late wife, Davy, at Oxford University. In his final book, *The Little Lost Marion and Other Mercies*, Vanauken recounted a more private chapter in Davy's life.

At age fourteen, long before Davy met Vanauken, she had given birth to a baby girl and placed her with adoptive parents. But Davy had never stopped loving the blue-eyed baby she had given up. Following Davy's death in the 1950s, Vanauken began searching for the child, whom Davy had named Marion. In 1988 he finally found her, now a young woman who resembled his beloved wife.

Meeting Davy's daughter, who was married and the mother of three children, gave Vanauken a greater insight into what he calls a "wholeness of vision" regarding abortion.

In *The Little Lost Marion* Vanauken writes: "Had the frightened young girl who was Davy lived in this decade instead of that remote one, she would perhaps have confided in a school counselor, who quite likely would have told her of the possibility of a quick and easy abortion. . . . What frightened fourteen-year-old would not clutch at the way out that the . . . counselor held out to her?"

But a wholeness of vision requires looking beyond the immediate concerns of a crisis pregnancy to the full and future implications of abortion. To achieve this, Vanauken writes, "I must see not only the frightened fourteen-year-old Davy . . . but also the warmly alive Marion and her family."

Each new being begins when information coming from the father with the sperm comes upon the information coming from the mother in the egg. As no other information will enter later on into the zygote, the fertilized egg, one is forced to admit that all the necessary and sufficient information to define that particular creature is found together at fertilization.

Jerome Lejeune, *The Concentration Can*

This is especially poignant in light of the fact that Davy and Vanauken had no children of their own. If Davy had aborted Marion, there would now be no loving woman who would call Vanauken father, and her three children would not exist.

"I glimpse," Vanauken writes, "what [John] Donne meant in saying that any man's death diminished him. I should be diminished if half a century ago Davy had clutched at the straw of abortion. And all the folk who have touched or shall touch the lives of Marion and her children and their children-to-be would be diminished."

Every abortion represents the loss of an individual: a person. It's a message we need somehow to communicate to those who are considering aborting other Marions.

Each abortion is a tragic loss; one that diminishes us all.

Q 68: *Pro-life advocates often compare America's abortion-on-demand policy to the Nazi Holocaust. Isn't that extreme?*

The comparison no doubt makes abortion advocates bridle, but pro-life advocates are not alone in seeing the connection.

Not too long ago the eight judges of Germany's Constitutional Court stood resplendent in their red satin robes as the chief justice read its most important decision in decades: The court struck down Germany's liberal abortion law, which was passed as a compromise between East and West German laws.

Under communism East Germany had embraced abortion on demand. In order to compromise, West Germany accepted a law that was significantly more permissive than its own law had been.

Immediately the new compromise law faced challenges to its constitutionality. And therein lies a fascinating story:

Germany's constitution dates back to the end of World War II and was explicitly designed to prevent another holocaust. The Nazis had tried to justify their use of the gas chambers on the grounds that some lives are not worth living and that therefore it is morally and legally permissible to snuff them out.

To stand against that idea, the German constitution includes a right-to-life clause stating that "everyone shall have the right to life and to physical inviolability." And the Constitutional Court exists to review all federal legislation and to ensure that no law overrides the right to life.

That explains the court's decision to strike down Germany's new abortion law. The judges declared that the constitution "obliges the state to protect human life" and that "the unborn are part of human life."

In ruling this way, the court was following a historical precedent from 1975. In that year the court struck down another permissive abortion law, invoking the right-to-life clause of the constitution and arguing that the "bitter experience" of the Nazi period gives historical evidence of what can happen when the right to life is not an absolute priority.

What makes the German debate so interesting is the fact that American pro-lifers are using exactly the same arguments on this side of the Atlantic. They argue that abortion rests on the same principle that undergirded the Nazi Holocaust: the idea that some human lives are not worthy of living, that it is morally and legally permissible to snuff them out.

In abortion, of course, that applies to unborn babies. But once people accept that principle, it can be applied equally well to other groups. As Francis Schaeffer once wrote, "If the fetus gets in the way, ditch it. If the old person gets in the way, ditch it. If you get in the way . . ." And the result could well be an American version of the Holocaust.

Naturally this argument drives pro-choice activists mad. They steadfastly refuse to see any connection between abortion and Nazism. But they ought to tune in to the debate going on in Germany. Many of the same people who lived through the Holocaust see clearly what's at stake. The same right-to-life principle that prohibits abortion also prevents another holocaust.

After all, the Holocaust did not start with gas chambers. It started when ordinary people accepted the *principle* that it is permissible to take an innocent human life.

The late Mother Teresa stated clearly and frankly the moral seriousness of abortion: "The greatest destroyer of peace today is abortion," she said at a National Prayer Breakfast in Washington, D.C. "It is a war against the child." Standing before the president and vice president, before congressional leaders and dignitaries from around the world, Mother Teresa continued, "If we accept that a mother can kill even her own child, how can we tell other people not to kill each other?"

Q 69: *If a young woman has an abortion, then "that's that," and she and the father can get on with life. Right?*

Wrong. There is increasing evidence that abortion is often traumatic and distressing. A survey by the *Los Angeles Times* found that more than half of the women who have had an abortion feel "a sense of guilt." More than one-fourth say they "mostly regret the abortion."

Because we tend to think of abortion as a women's issue, we often forget that every abortion involves a man as well. In fact, the same *Los Angeles Times* survey found that an even higher percentage of *fathers* of aborted children experience feelings of guilt and regret. Two-thirds of the fathers said they felt guilt over the abortion; more than a third reported feelings of regret.

Let me tell you about one group of people grieving over abortion. A hundred people had gathered together, most of them to mourn the deaths of their own children—children who had died through abortion. That grieving group included many men. Among them was Greg, who stood before the group crying. The two roses he carried trembled as he explained in a soft voice that they were in memory of his two sons—who were dead.

In his booklet *Men and Abortion,* Wayne Brauning, leader of Men's Abortion Recovery Ministries, describes a survey showing that fathers experience the same negative post-abortion reactions that women do: anger, depression, guilt, and broken relationships. A man who pressured a woman into having an abortion and drove her to the clinic can wake up months or years later and suddenly realize he delivered his own child over to death. It can be a terrible blow.

One of the men interviewed for Brauning's study—we'll call him George—says he now realizes he was just "too insecure and wimpy" to take a stand against his girlfriend's decision to have an abortion. Jack, another man surveyed, says that men who stand by while their own children are aborted are "spineless and gutless." Jack knows. He did the same thing himself.

These days when one of his friends is considering abortion as an option, Jack tells him to stop and think: "Imagine saying to your child, 'I'm footloose and fancy-free and I know they're going to kill you but, hey, don't slow me down.' What kind of father would say that?" Jack demands. "Not a real man. Being a man means you assume responsibility."

No matter how you look at it, a male who pushes a female into an abortion *knows* he's taking the coward's way out. And a female who goes along with the decision will grieve over it for the rest of her life.

Q 70: *Why do organizations such as Planned Parenthood insist that abortion should be readily available?*

Tragically abortion has become an industry. And what passes as abortion "counseling" in Planned Parenthood clinics is really marketing.

In a survey of women who had had abortions, some 90 percent said that the counseling they received gave few facts and was heavily biased in favor of abortion.

Take Kathy Walker. Her story is not unusual. Kathy was pregnant when she was thirteen. Her parents took her to a Planned Parenthood clinic, where the staff presented abortion as the only viable option. The doctor even warned Kathy in ominous tones that if she kept the baby, she'd end up a perpetual welfare mother.

Well, Kathy "chose" an abortion—but it could hardly be called an informed choice.

Carol Everett, who once owned and operated four lucrative abortion clinics, tells how the system works from the inside. If a girl decides to carry her baby to term, Carol explains, clinics don't make any money. They make money only if she has an abortion. So, inevitably, clinics put pressure on women to abort.

It starts with the first phone call. Nita Whitten, who once worked in an abortion clinic, says she was trained by a professional marketing firm in how to sell abortion over the phone. When a girl calls, Nita says, the object is not to help her; it's to "hook the sale."

The main tactic abortion clinics use is fear. The phone operator asks the girl how late her period is and then tells her, "You're pregnant." Not "You might be pregnant," but "You *are* pregnant."

They don't tell you that . . . the abortion industry is worth $90 billion plus.

Sara E. Hinlicky, "Their Well-kept Secrets about Abortion"

Once the girl comes into the clinic, the tactic is to present abortion as the ideal solution. Is the girl afraid to tell her parents? "They don't need to know," she's told.

Is she worried about school? "An abortion will let you stay in school."

Is she afraid she can't get the money? "Baby food and diapers cost a whole lot more."

And *after* the girl undergoes an abortion, there's even a marketing strategy to turn her into a repeat customer: Give her free birth-control pills.

That's right. A girl on the pill is more likely to be sexually active. But since young people often do not remember to take pills consistently, it's a good bet the girl will come back pregnant again.

As Carol Everett puts it, birth control sells abortions.

Abortion is a business. A big business that uses slick marketing tools.

Q 71: *Mom, I think I'm pregnant. What should I do? Do I keep my baby?*

If your teenager ever asks this, what will your reaction be?

I beg you to help your daughter choose life for her unborn child.

If your family cannot provide all the love and support the baby will need, please don't deny the baby life. In the midst of these difficult and painful circumstances you have a profound opportunity to demonstrate to your daughter, your friends, and your neighbors what true sacrificial Christian love really looks like. Encourage your daughter to think of the future her child deserves. God knows the plans he has for that child, and you and your daughter have a chance to participate with God in fulfilling those plans.

If you and your daughter choose life for her baby—and you must— you have several alternatives. If your daughter is older, she and the baby's father may decide to marry and keep the child. Or she might choose to keep the baby and either raise it on her own or continue to live with you, perhaps while she finishes school and finds employment. Especially if your daughter is young, marrying and/or keeping the baby may not be the best option. In that case, adoption can be a positive alternative.

As Christians each of us became children of our heavenly Father through adoption. It is the way he chose to make us a part of his family. What a priceless gift it can be to offer a child to a couple who have yearned and prayed—often for years—for a family, for the opportunity to share their love and God's love with a little one.

In recent years birth mothers have had the option of placing their child through open adoption, in which they choose the couple who will adopt their baby and are able to maintain some level of contact with them and the child as he or she grows up. This contact ranges from receiving photographs of the child once or twice a year to being present at birthday parties and exchanging Christmas gifts. One family invites their adopted children's birth mothers to spend an evening in their home during the Christmas season. The children make Christmas ornaments with their birth mothers' names on them, and they spend time hanging those on the tree together.

Open adoption allows the birth family to choose a couple who shares their faith, their philosophy of child rearing, and common interests. But even if a birth mother is not comfortable with the idea of open adoption (it may not be the best choice for everyone), placing a child in a loving home is a way to live redemptively in a culture that has devalued human life.

It is painful to contemplate placing a child for adoption—and even more painful to actually give the child up. But it is not nearly as painful or costly as the anguish of dealing with the emotional and physical consequences of abortion. Whether your daughter chooses to raise the baby herself or place it with an adoptive family, she will need all the love, support, and encouragement you can give. But you will reap the blessing and comfort of knowing that you and your daughter have given a precious child the loving, priceless gift of life.

Q 72: *But what about situations where tests show that the baby has birth defects?*

Eugenics—the practice of weeding out "defectives" and upgrading our genetic stock—was fashionable among progressives in the first half of the twentieth century. Margaret Sanger, founder of Planned Parenthood, called unabashedly for the elimination of "human weeds"— "morons, misfits, and the maladjusted"—and urged the sterilization of "genetically inferior races."

Of course Hitler's death camps for "inferior races" revealed where eugenics leads, and advocates dropped such offensive language. Yet today eugenics is returning in new forms. Thanks to advanced technology and the easy accessibility of abortion, it is no longer limited to progressive elites. It has quietly entered the mainstream.

For example, when testing reveals a Down's syndrome baby, doctors and insurance companies often pressure parents to abort, warning that the first year of life will cost $100,000. Not surprisingly, nine out of ten parents give in. One study revealed that a third of the mothers said they felt "more or less forced" to abort.

If doctors miss a few defective babies *before* birth, some recommend letting them die *after* birth. A 1975 poll found that 77 percent of American pediatric surgeons favor withholding food and medical treatment from Down's syndrome newborns. Some are doing just that, as we know from the 1982 Baby Doe case in Indiana.

Ironically, eugenics is returning just as medicine is making it possible for most Down's syndrome children to lead fairly normal lives—attend school, hold jobs, live independently. There's even a waiting list of couples wanting to adopt these children.

What do these couples know that doctors don't? They know children like my grandson Max. Max is an energetic six-year-old with blue eyes and blond hair that tosses as he bounces in my office chair shouting, "Grandpa's chair!" I love to take him to McDonald's and watch him clamber on the bright slides. From his flushed cheeks and quick smile I can easily see he's having the best time of all the kids there.

There's another way Max stands out. He is autistic and exhibits characteristic symptoms—attention difficulties, distant stares, and delayed development in walking and talking. But he has taught our family that these children, too, are a gift from God.

Max has an extraordinary capacity for love. When he was two, Patty and I took him to deliver Christmas gifts for Angel Tree, Prison Fellowship's ministry to children of prisoners. On the way we discussed our intention to demonstrate God's love to the two little girls whose daddy was in prison. Max sat sucking his thumb with his detached stare. But when we arrived, Max ran and embraced the two startled girls, first one and then the other. We were stunned. He usually shies away from strangers. But the toddler had understood our discussion and was determined to show those girls God's love!

When Max was first diagnosed, I agonized for my daughter, Emily. But she has risen to the challenge. On Max's sixth birthday she wrote me a letter: "I imagine that when God created Max, he took him straight from his heart, cupped him in his hands, and set him down on this earth." But "God knew that Max would need extra help. So God keeps his hands cupped around him. How could a child who is held by God be anything but a gift?"

Max reminds us that "God does not define us by our limitations and shortcomings," Emily added. If he did, where would any of us be? Some of us are handicapped genetically, others by injury or illness or crippling emotional pain. Kids like Max are a reminder that all of us experience the Fall in some way and need God's redeeming grace.

Raising a child with special needs is not easy—especially for people like Emily, who is a single parent. But the experience has transformed my little girl into a mature Christian woman. It has also made us more staunchly pro-life. I've always found the moral arguments for the sanctity of life compelling. But more compelling by far is the smile on a little boy's face as he jumps up and down squealing, "Grandpa's chair!"

To teens and parents asking questions about babies with disabilities, I say, "Get to know a child like Max."

Q 73: *But without abortion, wouldn't we soon have overpopulation?*

To hear the critics of the pro-life position talk, you might think so. *Washington Post* columnist Judy Mann wrote that the homeless children dying in Third World countries are the result of the church's "unthinking pro-family polices." Syndicated columnist Georgie Anne Geyer warned darkly that church teachings could "lead to the death of us all."

The premise here is that the more children a nation has, the poorer it will be. But if you look around the globe, the pattern is precisely the opposite. Rich countries often have high population densities while famine and poverty are much more common in sparsely populated countries like Somalia, Ethiopia, and the Sudan.

The population scare-mongers are operating from a faulty philosophy. They see every child as a mouth to feed—and nothing more. From their perspective every time a child is born, we all end up with a smaller slice of the pie.

But this is incredibly shortsighted. As children grow older, they don't just eat pies, they can bake new ones. They can add to society's pool of labor and creativity. And it is human creativity (or "capital") that determines whether a nation is rich or poor.

Human capital constantly finds better ways to grow food—so that today it takes only 3 percent of the American workforce to grow enough food for the entire nation. Human capital develops new ways to locate natural resources. Since 1950 the known reserves of iron have increased more than 1,000 percent as we develop better ways to locate and extract it. Human capital finds new ways to be productive with old resources. For example, the silicon in a computer chip is made from ordinary sand.

The real cause of poverty is not people but sin and oppression. The number one cause of hunger in the world today is war, followed closely by political corruption and centralized economic control.

Political leaders don't want to admit that their own misguided policies are holding people down. So they scapegoat families for having more children than the prescribed number. They chastise the church for welcoming children as gifts of God. They call on the government to seize control of the economy.

Leaders who respond this way don't seem to realize that what they're doing will only suppress human creativity—in the end creating more poverty and bringing what they fear down on their heads.

Abortion is not a solution to poverty. The mentality that sees death as a solution to the world's problems actually fosters those problems and, in fact, can only make them worse.

Q 74: *What about genetic engineering? Is it good or bad?*

In giving us an understanding of genetics through scientific research, God has entrusted to humankind a tremendous gift. As with any gift, we can put it to good or destructive use.

Geneticists often misrepresent many bad purposes as good ones. In fact, we should actively oppose much of what people want to do with genetic engineering.

An example of the good side of genetic research is the Human Genome Project, headed by Francis Collins, an evangelical Christian. The project seeks to identify the purpose for each strand of human DNA—to map the human genetic code. For Collins the science of genetics "is a form of worship in understanding God's creation." He sees genetic screening—testing for genetic abnormalities—as a powerful tool for alleviating suffering and saving lives.

But genetic screening can easily be taken beyond therapy and used in the service of eugenics, taking a consumerist approach to reproduction.

This is not some scary science-fiction prediction for the future. Scientists have identified many genetically based diseases that as yet have no known treatment. As a result, the most frequent use of genetic screening is to test babies in the womb—and to abort those who are defective. As Collins puts it, couples seeking genetic counseling often have a "new car mentality": If the baby isn't perfect, "you take it back to the lot and get a new one."

We're not talking here about racial or political eugenics—the kind discussed in the previous question. Instead, we might call it commercial eugenics: Parents act like consumers who treat their babies as merchandise that must fit certain specifications.

Ironically, the bad use of genetic screening is actually making it harder to practice the good use. By aborting defective babies, we're in essence saying that genetically imperfect people have no right to live. And if they have no right to live, why are we working so hard to find genetic cures for them?

Christians must never forget that God is not interested in physical and genetic perfection; he's interested in moral perfection. Throughout history, societies have suffered much more because of the evil schemes of *morally* defective people than because of those who are physically defective.

As Francis Collins says, genetics should be about ending suffering. It should not be about ending lives.

Q 75: *Then what about cloning?*

We've all seen pictures of Dolly, the cloned sheep. But what is really frightening is the fact that scientists have already applied these same techniques to human beings.

Researchers at George Washington University took human embryos consisting of only two to eight cells, split the cells apart, and allowed each cell to develop on its own. If each cell had been implanted in a woman's womb, the result would have been several genetically identical babies.

Why would anyone want several identical twins? The answer reads like science fiction. Some scientists have suggested freezing the extra embryos for future use. For example, if the original child dies at an early age, a frozen twin could be thawed out, and the parents could raise a clone identical to the child they lost. If the original child needs an organ transplant, just unfreeze a twin and use it for spare parts. The tissues would match perfectly.

Some geneticists even propose a catalog allowing parents to select their baby before birth. Parents could peruse photographs of the original children, pick one they like, buy a frozen clone, and raise an identical child. Some entrepreneurs could even specialize in embryos that grow up to be Einsteins or Picassos.

Does all of this sound far-fetched? It's not. America already has sperm banks for Nobel Prize winners and champion athletes. In short, we already have a market for preselected babies.

The only real barrier to mass-producing babies through cloning is a residual sense of the biblical worldview, which regards each person as valuable in his or her own right. But that worldview is under severe attack. Consider the words of geneticist Robert Haynes: "For three thousand years," he says, "a majority of people have considered that human beings were special. . . . It's the Judeo-Christian view of man. Well, not anymore," Haynes declares. Genetics teaches that "we are biological machines" and nothing more.

This is the philosophy of genetic reductionism, which treats people as nothing more than DNA on legs. Put into practice, it manipulates, uses, and discards the human body as if it were an industrial product.

Again, Christians support science as the investigation of God's world. But we must make sure that we apply science in a way that furthers God's purposes. Genetic technology can be a great benefit, or it can be a Pandora's box of horrors—depending on the worldview that guides it.

Q 76: If people want to die, isn't it more merciful to let them commit suicide than to allow them to suffer?

Those who support doctor-assisted suicide—allowing doctors to prescribe lethal doses of drugs to terminally ill patients—claim that the taboo against it is nothing but a vestige of religious prejudice.

Ironically, it was a pagan culture, not a Christian one, that first prohibited doctors from killing their patients. In traditional and tribal cultures, as Nigel Cameron explains in his book *The New Medicine: Life and Death after Hippocrates,* suicide was a common practice. The person most likely to provide the deadly drugs was the medicine man, the witch doctor, the sorcerer. The power to cure also meant the power to kill.

But a major turning point occurred roughly four hundred years before Christ when the philosophers of ancient Greece enunciated the Hippocratic oath. For the first time doctors pledged never to use their medicinal arts for killing. They promised: "I will give no deadly drug, [even] if asked for it." The Hippocratic oath turned medicine into the first "profession," as doctors "professed" a set of moral standards.

When Christianity came on the scene, the church fathers embraced the Hippocratic oath and adapted it to biblical ethics. For two thousand years the medical profession was a complex fabric of technical skills bound together by moral commitments.

But today that fabric is unraveling. Medicine is losing its moral dimension and is being reduced to only a set of technical skills applied in the service of social engineering.

Just consider the Netherlands, which entered the brave new world of euthanasia (assisted suicide) several years ago. Within a short time, Dutch doctors moved beyond patient requests and began making decisions on their own about who should live or die. Today nearly half of Dutch doctors say they've given lethal injections *without* the patient's knowledge or consent.

Clearly the ancient Hippocratic oath, with its taboo against killing, was no mere "religious prejudice." It was based on a profound understanding of the temptation that doctors face with their power over life and death.

But today that taboo is crumbling. Oregon voters have decided to let doctors kill as well as cure, and similar bills are under consideration in several other states. The U.S. Supreme Court has declined to rule that patients have a constitutional right to assisted suicide, but their decision contained ominous language suggesting that the court might change its mind once it could see how assisted suicide worked out in practice.

Perhaps the greatest tragedy is that patients who request suicide are typically motivated not by illness but by loneliness and depression. What they really need is not a deadly drug but care and companionship.

The acceptance of doctor-assisted suicide signals not only the end of medicine as a morally based profession but also a profound failure of our own character—a failure to commit ourselves to loving and caring for the sick, the handicapped, and the dying.

So even the basic question of euthanasia presents a challenge to all of us, parents and children alike: Will we allow doctors to do away with the weakest members of the human community? Or will we muster the moral will to stand by those weaker members with love and care?

As our question implies, euthanasia supporters claim that when people are suffering, helping them kill themselves is the only "compassionate" thing to do—just as the abortion lobby says that when babies are unwanted, abortion is the "compassionate" choice for them as well.

Do no harm.

Hippocrates

These definitions of compassion are cheap substitutes for the real thing. It's easy to hook up a terminally ill person to an IV full of lethal drugs. *Real* compassion is caring for him for months or even years— and as the late Mother Teresa put it so well, "letting him see Jesus in the midst of his suffering."

KEY POINTS IN BRIEF

✓ The human fetus is a person and should have all the legal protections given to every other person.

✓ Germany's Constitutional Court has recognized the valid analogy between abortion-on-demand and the Holocaust. We are suffering through our own massacre of the innocents.

✓ Both young mothers and fathers suffer grievously because of their decision to abort their unborn child. Abortion is not a "quick and easy" solution in any way.

✓ Planned Parenthood and other pro-abortion organizations help to make abortion a multibillion-dollar industry.

✓ Adoption is an incomparably better solution to an unplanned "crisis" pregnancy than abortion.

✓ Famines and other shortages of critical supplies are most often the result of war, political corruption, and the centralized control of economies. Many densely populated countries realize the advantages of human creativity and are some of the wealthiest regions in the world. Not only is abortion not necessary as a means of fighting overpopulation, but the economic premises of the overpopulation scare-mongers are dead wrong.

✓ Our contemporary understanding of genetics may, in the long run, be a great boon to humanity. Today, however, it too often becomes a means of promoting consumerist eugenics resulting in the death of many handicapped children in the womb.

✓ Assisted suicide is directly contrary to Christian teaching.

CHAPTER 10
Guess What I Learned Today?
Schools, Values, and Violence

Q 77: *Public schools can't teach religion, so you can't expect too much from them, can you?*

Actually, the public schools sometimes do teach non-Christian religions—in disguise. Friends of mine saw their five-year-old withdraw into a corner, sit absolutely still, her hands folded, her eyes closed. For a lively little girl, this was unusual behavior, and her mother was puzzled.

"Stephanie, what are you doing? Stephanie!"

Finally the little girl opened her eyes. She explained it was an activity she had learned at school. And she went on to describe what her mother recognized as classic Eastern meditation.

Stephanie was in a program called PUMSY in Pursuit of Excellence. Pumsy is a cute, fairy-tale dragon who discovers a wise guide named Friend, who teaches Pumsy that her mind is like a pool of water: There's a muddy mind, which tempts her to think negative thoughts, and a Clear Mind, which can solve all her problems through positive thinking. Friend tells Pumsy, "Your Clear Mind is the best friend you'll ever have. . . . It is always close to you, and it will never leave you."

This sounds suspiciously like religious language: "I will never leave you nor forsake you" (Josh. 1:5). And a few pages later in the story, we read, "You have to trust [your Clear Mind] and let it do good things for you."

This "mind" sounds like divine power.

And that's exactly what it is. The Pumsy story is just a fairy-tale way of teaching Hinduism.

In Hinduism the individual self is known by the name *atman,* and the universal spirit is known by the name *Brahma.* In the New Age version, Brahma becomes the "higher self." The purpose of using meditation, myths, and mantras is to achieve a state of enlightenment in which we realize our true identity as part of God. (The "Clear Mind" Stephanie was taught about is a euphemism for the divine spark within.)

As New Agers put it, we connect with the "higher self" and tap into it for energy, creativity, and wisdom.

New Age programs often soft-pedal Eastern spirituality, however, and are marketed to schools and business as simply psychological techniques to enhance creativity, boost productivity, and unleash inner potential.

The philosophy of the school room in one generation will be the philosophy of the government in the next.

Abraham Lincoln

However, if you are aware of the New Age worldview, you can spot the hidden assumptions. For example, guided imagery exercises can be ways of putting an imaginary face on the universal spirit to "hear" its wisdom.

In short, these are not merely neutral psychological techniques. They're spiritual practices, and they may well tap into alien and dangerous spiritual realms.

These programs purport to be teaching kids to look within to solve their problems, to be more self-reliant. PUMSY teaches youngsters to chant slogans like "I can handle it," "I can make it happen," and "I am me, I am enough."

But there's that religious language again—like God's name in the

Old Testament: I am who I am. What PUMSY teaches is not self-esteem; it's self-worship.

Educational programs like PUMSY are popping up all across the country. The advertising may say it's a program in self-esteem or drug education or whatever. Teachers often don't even recognize the underlying philosophy. So it's up to parents to find out what their children are learning, to teach them to discern true from false religion, and to equip them with spiritual weapons to fight the spiritual battle.

Q 78: *My school is so anti-Christian—what can I do about it?*

It is true that many schools display what appears to be an anti-Christian bias. We live in what historically has been a Christian culture, so some administrators bend over backward not even to mention the meaning of Christmas, for example. There is an almost obsessive fear that doing so will offend someone. But our job is to be loving as we educate padministrators and teachers to be sure that the school officials at least are not playing fast and loose with history.

My own daughter, for example, discovered that in her son's school Kwanza was being celebrated but the Christian aspects of Christmas were being largely ignored. She researched the background of Kwanza and discovered that it is not some sacred African ritual but a celebration of very recent origin, a celebration invented by a California professor. My daughter challenged the teachers and ended up insisting that her son not participate in the Kwanza festivities. This is a great way to educate teachers, most of whom do not know the background of Kwanza. There is no way to make it the equivalent of what we celebrate at Christmas—the birth of Jesus.

When I have read textbooks with my grandchildren, I have discovered errors—sometimes serious ones and ones with anti-Christian bias. My grandchildren have had some success in arguing these issues with their teachers. I know of many Christian parents who have pointed out other errors or challenged practices that discriminate against Christians. Often they succeed.

These aren't isolated personal illustrations. From all across the country we have heard from parents who have successfully challenged school boards and teachers, the overwhelming majority of whom are not hostile to Christianity as such but are simply caught up in this cultural desire to offend no one.

Parents can make a difference. Just look at what happened in Kansas when concerned parents petitioned the school board to open up state standards so that both sides of the evolution-creation debate could be taught in schools. Although the media made it appear that the school board was banning the teaching of evolution, the board did exactly the reverse. They took away the state requirement that teachers would have to tell students that Darwinian macroevolution is a fact beyond dispute, which of course it is not; it is hotly disputed in scientific terms. The board's decision meant simply that both points of view can be taught. So contrary to the media, the board actually voted for an increased coverage of the topic in the state's science curriculum guidelines. In doing so, they took a stand for academic freedom and afforded protection against indoctrination.

Sometimes teenagers and parents have had to resist what clearly becomes oppression. One good illustration is what happened in Calvert County, Maryland, where a senior named Julie Schenk asked to lead a prayer at her high school graduation. Of course it's perfectly legal for students to lead classmates in prayer, even though it would not be legal for school personnel to do so. But all too often, schools refuse to allow students to pray for fear of provoking a pricey ACLU lawsuit. And sure enough, a graduate named Nick Becker objected to the prayer. The ACLU swooped in to back him up—and school officials backed down.

Julie was told that instead of a prayer, she could invite the graduates and their families to participate in thirty seconds of "silent reflection."

It turned out to be the noisiest "silent reflection" in history. When Julie asked the crowd to stand and begin the reflection, a man in the audience began to pray out loud: "Our Father, who art in heaven . . ."

Instantly, large numbers of the four thousand parents and students in attendance joined in the prayer until it echoed all over the auditorium. Nick Becker, the student who had objected to prayer in the first place, stormed out of the building.

> *I am much afraid that schools will prove to be the great gates of hell unless they diligently labor in explaining the Holy Scriptures, engraving them in the hearts of youth.*
>
> Martin Luther, quoted in *The Rebirth of America*

There is no excuse for us not to be familiar with what the law permits, to learn about our own Christian history, to understand what is wrong with much of what is being taught and pressed on our young people. Then we must challenge school officials or teachers when the facts clearly support us. Most of the time, if we present our case in a loving and winsome way, we can reverse what seems to be hostility to the Christian faith. More often than not, such resistance is the result of ignorance or pressures of political correctness. If the resistance succeeds, it's usually because we haven't done our job.

Q 79: *My school hands out condoms. If kids are going to have sex, isn't it important for them to practice safe sex?*

Handing out condoms in school—especially without any counseling and without parents' consent—gives students no inducement to do any serious thinking about sexual activity and its risks.

Much sex education today is aimed at making sexual activity a common experience devoid of deep meaning. Sex educators are worried that teens tend to treat sex as passionate, romantic, meaningful—that they get swept away by their feelings. These educators believe that teens are more likely to use birth control and condoms if sex is treated clinically, stripping it of its meaning.

Sex without significance. No commitment, no emotional involvement, simple animal pleasure.

What an incredible irony: In trying to teach young people to be responsible, public schools have adopted an irresponsible philosophy of sex. The only controls on sexual behavior that schools promote are utilitarian: Don't get pregnant; don't get AIDS.

Here, have a condom.

It's preposterous to think that this approach to sex education can teach kids responsibility. Do we teach any other subject that way? It's like teaching driver's education by not mentioning any traffic laws and then counseling kids to practice "safe driving" by wearing seat belts. It's like teaching football by ignoring the rules of the game and telling kids to practice "safe sports" by wearing pads.

The truth is that educators have abdicated their responsibility for moral training. They've given up. We can't stop kids from having sex, the argument goes; the only thing we can do is help make it safe.

By that logic, *Commonweal* magazine says, schools might just as well offer supervised sex. Provide students with clean, monitored bedrooms, with condoms discreetly placed on nearby nightstands.

Outlandish as it sounds, some parents have actually come to the same conclusion. The *Washington Post* interviewed several parents who allow their children to invite partners home for sex. The kids are going to do it anyway, the parents say; at least they're safer in their own home.

The sad thing is that it doesn't have to be this way. Studies show that teens do care what their parents think. They are receptive to moral guidance. Sex-education programs that teach morality have been well received.

That should come as no surprise. Teens are just like the rest of us: They respond positively to a challenge; they are attracted to adults who expect a lot of them, who believe in them.

Sex isn't the equivalent of a volleyball game. Our teens already know this, even if some of their educators have forgotten it. Teens respect adults who know it too. You can talk to your teenagers about how unwise (and morally wrong) it is to have sex before marriage. You can point out that free condom distribution in the schools is misguided and endorses a point of view that can only make worse the problems these programs propose to remedy.

Q 80: *The textbooks (or the teachers) say so. They must know more than you, right?*

One of the joys of being a grandparent is helping your grandchildren with their homework. But when I helped my ten-year-old grand-daughter, Caroline, she learned a lesson. So did I—a sobering one.

Caroline had just finished her first day of fifth grade, and together we leafed through her brand-new, glossy history textbook. In a section on the Bill of Rights, we came upon a caption: "The Bill of Rights promised individual freedom to many people—but not to women, blacks, and Native Americans."

Before I could respond, Caroline burst out, "That's not fair!"

"The book is wrong," I replied. "That simply isn't so."

Caroline told me I was wrong. She knew the Bill of Rights discriminates, she said, "because the book says so."

There was only one way to convince Caroline that the caption was wrong. Together, we turned to the Bill of Rights and read it aloud.

We read Article 1, which guarantees the right of "the people" to practice their religion freely. We read Article 2, which protects the right of "the people" to keep and bear arms.

After reading each amendment, I asked Caroline, "Does that article exclude women, blacks, or Native Americans?" Each time she shook her head because every bill referred to "people," meaning all people.

After we had read the Tenth Amendment, Caroline looked at me in amazement. "You're right! The book is wrong."

I wish I could say that my granddaughter's textbook is an isolated example of historical revisionism. But it is not; it is symptomatic of an epidemic. It's an attempt to rewrite the American story and character to promote current political ideology.

"Politically correct" criticism of the American past seeks to redress what cultural elites believe are "oppressive Western thought forms" used by the majority to dominate blacks, women, and other minorities. Much of what is called multiculturalism is therefore nothing but an excuse for an anti-Western diatribe.

The purpose of many people in the media and in our colleges and in some private institutions is clear: to capture the minds of the rising generation, to achieve their own relativistic agenda by alienating the young from their heritage.

We cannot permit the political revisionism of our past. Why? Because a crucial way civilizations pass on a sense of identity to succeeding generations is by conveying a true remembrance of their historical heritage. That's why Old Testament prophets constantly reminded the Israelites of God's mighty acts in history.

When our children are taught the truth about our history, naturally they'll regret some of America's failures, but they'll also admire what America has achieved, and they'll gain respect for our heritage—their heritage.

My granddaughter's experience with a politically correct textbook reminds us that vigilance is indeed the price of liberty. So take a look at what your children or grandchildren are being taught about American history. One certain way our liberty could be quickly lost is through just this kind of distorted education.

Q 81: *Why have the public schools become so dangerous? What's gone wrong?*

In the aftermath of the Columbine High School massacre in Littleton, Colorado, everyone is frantically seeking answers: Politicians call for gun control; commentators decry the decadent popular culture; scientists even suggest genetic disorders. But the real answer goes much deeper—to a clash of worldviews. Dramatically displayed in the Littleton tragedy were two great worldviews competing for allegiance in today's world.

On one side was postmodernism, with its roots in the nihilism preached by Friedrich Nietzsche. The nineteenth-century German philosopher argued that the "language of good and evil" is rooted in neither truth nor reason but in the will to power. Half a century ago the Nazis fleshed out Nietzsche's ideas.

In Colorado those ideas once again revealed their horrific consequences as two teenagers displaying Nazi symbols and slogans mowed down their classmates in cold blood.

Underlying the killers' fascination with the imagery of power and destruction was the outright embrace of evil—what literary critic Roger Shattuck describes as an attitude of "approval toward moral and radical evil, as evidence of superior will and power."

Who could imagine that two alienated teens would take Nietzsche to heart? Yet the wrenching irony is that the surrounding adult culture has been similarly influenced by Nietzsche.

In the *Atlantic Monthly,* political scientist Francis Fukuyama contends that the decline in traditional morality in the West can be traced most directly to Nietzsche's view that morality is not objectively true—that people create their own values to reflect their interests.

This radical relativism took root on college campuses as postmodernism and deconstructionism and has now filtered down to the lower grades. In public schools, students are taught to "construct" their own truths and values. Teachers are trained not to offer any direction, lest they hamper a child's autonomy.

No wonder our schools are succumbing to a *Lord of the Flies* mentality. In this classic novel William Golding described the depravity to which even "good" kids can sink when left on their own without adult moral guidance. Today's kids receive little moral guidance because adults have abdicated their responsibility.

And not just in education. We have created a subculture that segregates children into a parallel world. Today many conscientious parents define their role less as interacting directly with their kids and more as managing their kids' involvement in peer-oriented groups. Kids spend so much time in day-care centers, sports groups, summer camps, and the mall that many bond more closely to their peers than to their parents. The market reinforces the segregation by offering teens their own movies, videos, music, and Internet games. News reports say the parents of the two Colorado killers were kind and caring, yet they allowed their kids to inhabit an eerie parallel world created by movies, Internet games, and the "Trenchcoat Mafia."

The inescapable lesson is that ideas do have consequences. Nietzsche's philosophy has shaped both the highbrow culture of academia and the lowbrow culture of alienated Internet skulkers. When the two cultures come together, as they did in Littleton, the result is explosive.

The other inescapable lesson is that parents cannot trust peer groups or even schools to espouse their parental value system. Parents must intervene, get involved in the lives of their kids, and find out what they're doing, how they're spending their time, what they're studying, what they're interested in. It is hard to believe that the parents of one of the Littleton killers did not even know that he was making a bomb in their own home. That should serve as a wake-up call for all of us.

Q 82: *I would never be violent, but I like to watch slash-'em-up movies. What harm can it do?*

Teenagers continually hear this message from those who profit most from violent entertainment. With all of the celebrated school shootings in recent years, Hollywood executives have been tripping over themselves to recall violent films and TV programs aimed at teenagers. Yet at the same time, Tinseltown is claiming with a straight face that there's absolutely no correlation between make-believe violence and the real thing.

Moviemakers argue that what's really responsible for murderous kids is, as one Hollywood executive put it, "bad home life, bad parenting, [and] having guns in the home."

But as writer Gregg Easterbrook points out in the *New Republic,* Hollywood is wrong.

For example, a University of Chicago Law School study reveals that the percentage of homes with guns has not changed noticeably since World War II. What has changed, Easterbrook notes, "is the willingness of people to fire their guns at one another."

Another study reveals that America's postwar murder rate began to rise roughly a decade after TV viewing became common in the 1950s. The same phenomenon occurred in South Africa. There, television was not generally available until 1975; the national murder rates began rising about a decade later.

Perhaps most damning of all are the findings of Leonard Eron, a psychologist who found that "those who watched the most TV and movies in childhood were much more likely to have been arrested for, or convicted of, violent felonies."

While violent entertainment might not spur the average adult to murder, for children and the psychologically unbalanced, Gregg Easterbrook says, "the calculus is different."

"Mass murders by the young, once phenomenally rare, are suddenly on the increase," Easterbrook writes. "Can it be a coincidence that this increase is happening at the same time that Hollywood has begun to market the notion that mass murder is fun?"

The evidence that what we feed our mind affects how we behave should come as no surprise to Christians. In Proverbs, we read that "as [a man] thinks in his heart, so is he" (Prov. 23:7, NKJV). And the apostle Paul exhorts us to dwell on what is true, noble, right, pure, lovely, and admirable (Phil. 4:8).

> *Television [video game, movie] violence by itself does not kill you. It destroys your violence immune system and conditions you to derive pleasure from violence. . . . When people are frightened or angry, they will do what they've been conditioned to do.*
>
> David Grossman and Mary Cagney, "Trained to Kill: Children Who Kill"

No matter what those Hollywood executives claim, there is a link between make-believe murder and the real thing. Mass murder is not fun, as the movies suggest. Just ask the families of Littleton, Colorado.

It is the height of folly for parents, particularly Christian parents, not to care about what their children watch on TV, the movies they see in the theaters, the music they listen to, the video games they play. It is indeed a matter of life and death.

Q 83: *I've just got to get the anger out of my system, don't I?*

In the movie *Analyze This,* a psychiatrist suggests to his patient, an angry mobster, that hitting a pillow will make him feel better. But instead of punching the pillow, the mobster pulls out a gun and shoots it. "So, do you feel better?" the psychiatrist asks.

"Yeah," says the mobster, smiling, "I do."

The scene is funny, but it perpetuates a widespread and erroneous notion that venting anger helps us get rid of it. Contrary to what we've all heard, psychologists are now finding that venting anger actually increases aggression.

Pop psychology has perpetuated the notion that "getting your anger out" is good for you—that it helps defuse rage. This is the theory of catharsis: that expressing an emotion or an urge helps to release it.

But new studies conducted at Iowa State University and at Case Western Reserve University found that venting anger actually makes people more aggressive. As reported in the *New York Times,* the studies found that human subjects who pummeled a punching bag became more aggressive than subjects who did not. As one researcher put it, "They keep trying to get this emotional release [through walloping a punching bag], but it never happens."

Instead, the opposite happens: Hitting things seems to give people "permission to relax their self-control," as the *New York Times* put it— and thus leads to escalating aggressiveness.

The theory of catharsis became popular through the psychological theories of Sigmund Freud. According to Freud, when anger is repressed, pressure builds up like steam in a kettle—and the best way to relieve the pressure is to release it by hitting a punching bag or smashing a piece of china.

Unfortunately, our culture has been slow to grasp the folly of this idea. In fact, "self-expression" of all kinds is usually seen as a good thing.

But the most recent findings of social science are now supporting the notion of self-restraint over self-expression. They confirm the biblical insight that giving in to our impulses is a bad idea.

Self-control, in fact, is part of the fruit of the Spirit, says the apostle Paul in his letter to the Galatians. And the apostle James warns Christians of the great damage we cause by not controlling our tongues.

Not that self-restraint is always easy. Any virtue—whether it's patience, joy, or chastity—must be practiced until it becomes a habit. Then it becomes part of our character, our instinctive way of responding.

When your teenager expresses the idea that releasing his or her anger is simply necessary, recognize this notion for what it is: wrong. Once again science is discovering that the biblical view of self-restraint is correct. Acting out anger only makes it worse—for whatever you act out, you are practicing. And whatever you practice, you grow better at doing.

What we ought to be practicing are the biblical virtues, and we should practice them until they become second nature. And then, when we act naturally, what people will see in us is the fruit of the Spirit.

Q 84: *I'm not into computer porn or anything. Why are you so uptight about my computer use?*

There's no running away from the challenges of the Information Age. As Thomas Friedman of the *New York Times* recently wrote, "The Internet has become inescapable, at least among the middle class. The way [we] communicate, invest, work and learn, is being fundamentally transformed by the Web."

What makes this ascendance particularly worrisome, says Friedman, is that the Internet comes with "no built-in editor, publisher, censor, or even filters." With one mouse click you can wander into a Nazi beer hall or a pornographer's library. The only really effective filters, he says, "are the values, knowledge and judgment that your kid brings to the Web in his or her own head and heart."

Friedman is right. The problem is, as Littleton taught us, we cannot rely on kids' having built-in filters. They have to be taught right from wrong. And these days many kids are raising themselves without any real moral guidance from the adults in their lives.

The combination of the wide-open world on-line and a culture where parents "spend less time building their kids' internal codes and filters" is, as Friedman notes, a "potentially dangerous cocktail."

The only way parents can safeguard their children from that hazardous "cocktail" is to do what good parents have always done: spend time with their kids, teaching them right from wrong and helping them to apply that knowledge in every situation—including when they're sitting alone at a computer.

The story of Tyler offers a case in point. At an auction last April, Tyler successfully bid on a 1955 Ford convertible, a Vincent van Gogh painting, antique furniture, and a replica of a Viking ship. All in all, he placed some three million dollars' worth of winning bids.

The problem is, Tyler is only thirteen years old, and his allowance is only fifteen dollars a week. He was able to make all those phony bids thanks to the Internet. In the end, the price his parents paid was only a little embarrassment, but their experience is a lesson on the challenges parents face in the Information Age.

Like many thirteen-year-olds, Tyler Andrews knows a lot about the Internet. One of his favorite sites is eBay, the Internet auction Web site. "They don't ask you for your credit card or any proof that you're over eighteen," Tyler told reporters.

Tyler first tried selling his best friend as a slave, but he didn't get any takers. That's when he decided to go on a shopping spree.

His parents first learned about the bids when they got a call from an auction house. When they recovered from their shock, they took away Tyler's Internet privileges.

As a parent, familiarize yourself with the world your kids inhabit. Learn how the Information Age works so that you can identify potential pitfalls ahead of time and protect and prepare your children.

This brave new technology offers both benefits and dangers, and you'd better be prepared for both—unless, of course, you've got room in the garage for a Viking ship, a Ford convertible, and anything else your computer-savvy kids may order through the Internet.

Q 85: *My best friend just died. I'm really messed up, and I need some help here. How do I get over my friend's death?*

The aftermath of the massacre at Columbine High School followed a predictable pattern: First came teams of police investigators. Then came the grief counselors, more than a hundred of them, ready to help the survivors deal with their anguish.

As it turned out, the counselors had no one to counsel. Not because the kids weren't grieving but because they were turning to a more effective grief counselor: the church.

Patrick Simington, like his schoolmates at Columbine High, was offered the services of professional grief counselors. But instead of talking to them, Patrick joined his friends at a memorial service at the Light of the World Roman Catholic Church, which has an active charismatic renewal movement. Four young members of that church were lost in the massacre.

Patrick's mother told the *Washington Times* that what is really helping him get through this crisis "is his faith."

Well, Patrick isn't unique. Columbine student Lauren Johnson's parents encouraged her to seek out a professional counselor. Instead, Laura turned to the staff at West Bowler Community Church—the home church of shooting victim Cassie Bernall. Johnson told reporters, "I just like it better this way," adding, "It seemed like most of the kids from the school were there."

As the *Washington Times* notes, "Many Columbine students are bypassing offers of secular therapy and turning instead to their churches." In fact, pastors and church youth leaders have been overwhelmed by kids, parents, and others coming for help.

As Chad Stafford, former pastor of the First Assembly of God church in Denver, explains, "Kids aren't wanting psychology at this time. . . . They want to know, 'Why did this happen?'" Grief counseling may give kids information, he adds, "but we're able to give them guidance."

Stafford is right. When young people are confronted firsthand with the need to grapple with issues of life and death, they need something more than permission to vent their feelings about their losses. Of course they need the freedom to grieve and to take time to share their pain, to openly acknowledge the awful reality of death. But they also want answers that offer hope and encouragement and the knowledge that this life and its often deep anguish are not all there is. They need help in doing something more than just "sort through their feelings."

> *Of all men, we [Christians] hope most of death; yet nothing will reconcile us to—well, its* unnaturalness. *We know that we're not made for it; we know how it crept into our destiny as an intruder; and we know Who defeated it. Because Our Lord is risen we know that on one level it is an enemy already disarmed; but because we know that the natural level also is God's creation we cannot cease to fight against the death which mars it.*

C. S. Lewis, *God in the Dock*

And this is where Christian parents can help. Show your kids from the Bible that death is not the end (John 14:2-3), and point them to the truth about the eternal life that Jesus Christ gives. When Jesus went to Bethany after his friend Lazarus died, he wept over the loss. But then he offered words of hope to Lazarus's grieving sisters: "I am the resurrection and the life. Those who believe in me . . . will live again. They are given eternal life for believing in me and will never perish" (John 11:25-26, NLT).

When secular grief counselors offer kids nothing more than the opportunity to vent negative emotions about their loss, who can blame kids for saying, "Thanks, but no thanks." If your kids are faced with the death of a friend or other person close to them, encourage them to search out the hope that only faith in Christ can provide.

Key Points in Brief

✓ Public schools sometimes stray into teaching religions contrary to Christianity. Parents need to be aware of what their children are learning and the worldview assumptions that underlie their lessons.

✓ When school counselors hand out condoms, they teach kids that sexuality is nothing more than animal pleasure. This is exactly the wrong message to be sending, and one that teens themselves don't buy into.

✓ Christians need to speak up when textbooks and other school materials present false views, especially when these are factually inaccurate.

✓ Contemporary violence in the schools, such as the Columbine High School massacre, demonstrates the cruel and evil power of false worldviews.

✓ Violent entertainment compromises our "immune system" to violence and influences us to respond with violence in our daily life. When Hollywood says this is untrue, the entertainment industry is only trying to protect its bottom line.

✓ Parents need to be aware of every aspect of their children's lives, especially the means they use to entertain themselves. The Internet and other mass media are inescapable concerns. Parents must help their children make wise entertainment choices, remembering that our whole life—including our recreation—is meant to transform us into the image of Christ.

✓ The death of a friend is often a tremendous blow to young people. At these times, especially, parents should direct their children to the hope we have in Christ.

CHAPTER 11

What Do I Owe the Government?
Government, Politics, and Citizenship

Q 86: Why do church people speak of America as a "Christian nation"?

The founding principles of America were strongly influenced by the Judeo-Christian tradition. Rather than call America a "Christian nation," which may imply a church-dominated state, it's more accurate to say that America is a nation profoundly influenced by Christian principles. Americans' beliefs have become far more diverse than they were in the days of the nation's founding, but the Christian principles still at work in our democratic institutions are the prime reason that those institutions do indeed work.

Our country's Judeo-Christian and classical Greek heritages influenced what governmental institutions were designed to do and not do. They provided the background for our understanding that the nation must be one of "laws, not men," as Oliver Wendell Holmes put it. Even the ideal of the "pursuit of happiness" comes from the Judeo-Christian tradition: The phrase describes the founders' longing for a society of corporate justice, not individual license. "Happiness," as used in the Declaration of Independence, means the pursuit of virtue (that is, goodness), not hedonism.

Another example: America's Founding Fathers were also influenced by the Judeo-Christian teaching about the human tendency to abuse power. So they adopted the principle of the separation of powers. Within the government, power was diffused through a system of checks and balances so that no one branch could dominate another. The Founders also assumed that what was then America's Christian consensus would be the most powerful brake on the natural avarice of government. Because of its Judeo-Christian heritage, America has avoided the worst effects of humankind's obsession with power.

Two other ideas—equality and the rule of law—are central to Western democracy, and they can be traced directly to our culture's Christian heritage as well.

Take equality. As every schoolchild knows, the United States was, in the words of Abraham Lincoln, "dedicated to the proposition that 'all men are created equal.' " Where did that idea come from? Christianity, of course. The Christian tradition is the reason that the Founders believed in something called "natural rights," that is, a belief that we possess certain rights simply because we are human beings endowed by our Creator with these rights. The Founders enumerated these rights as "life, liberty and the pursuit of happiness," which they saw as belonging to personhood itself. These rights are not dependent on the whim of the ruler—whether a king or a legislature—and they are not conferred on the people by themselves. They cannot be given or taken away, only honored or violated.

The idea of equality also proceeded from a Reformation doctrine known as *coram deo,* which means "the face of God." Reformer John Calvin taught that all men and women, regardless of social status, live their lives in the face of God. This meant that individuals did not have to approach God through either the church or the state. It relieved them from the oppressive power of tyrants. They stood before God in their full dignity as humans.

Crucially, the notion of *coram deo* led to the insistence that the state's role was limited. The state's role wasn't to rule over everybody but simply to ensure that the structures ordained by God—such as the family and the church—function properly. This idea of limited government was another core value of our democracy.

In Western democracy, equality means, more than anything else, equality before the law. And that brings us to the other great contribution of Christianity: the rule of law.

> ### *Religion in America takes no direct part in the government or society, but it must, nevertheless, be regarded as the foremost of the political institutions of that country.*
>
> Alexis de Tocqueville, *Democracy in America*

In the mid-seventeenth century, the Scottish clergyman Samuel Rutherford wrote a book that at the time was earth-shattering: It was entitled *Lex Rex,* which means "the law is king." Rutherford argued that ruler and ruled alike were subject to the same transcendent laws of God.

It's impossible to overstate how essential this idea is to American democracy. We are a nation of laws and not men. That is, we are governed by the laws to which we consent, and the law applies to everyone equally.

These two Christian ideas, *coram deo* and *lex rex,* influenced the Founders and enabled them to break free from the tyrannical rule of King George III. These ideas helped the Founders establish a model of government—of ordered liberty—that has been the envy of the world ever since.

When church people call America a "Christian nation," they mean that Christian ideas are at the heart of our democracy. This is true. But it's more accurate to say that America is a nation influenced by Christianity because the American state has never been controlled by the church and should not be.

Q 87: *Do Christians believe in the separation of church and state?*

Yes, Christians believe in the separation of church and state. In fact, it's disastrous for the church to reduce the gospel to a political agenda.

But some background on the original meaning of "separation of church and state" needs to inform our full answer.

The original meaning of the First Amendment, that Congress shall make no law "respecting an establishment of religion," was simply intended to keep Congress from preferring one religion over another, with the distinct possibility that individual states might choose to adopt state churches. Indeed, many of the individual states continued to support established expressions (official state churches) of the Christian faith well into the 1830s. The Constitution says nothing about "separation of church and state"—the phrase comes from a letter Thomas Jefferson wrote a decade after the Constitution was adopted.

In setting forth the First Amendment, the American Founders *sought to protect* religious freedom as the first liberty. They understood that without the liberty to express our most fundamental beliefs, all other liberties inevitably crumble.

But the point cannot be emphasized too strongly that the First Amendment was intended to protect the church from government interference; it in no way intended that religious influence should be kept out of public life. In fact, America's Founding Fathers were well aware that limited government could succeed only if there were an underlying consensus of values shared by the populace.

In 1798 John Adams eloquently acknowledged the understanding of our constitutional framers: "We have no government armed in power capable of contending with human passions unbridled by morality and religion. . . . Our constitution was made only for a moral and religious people. It is wholly inadequate for the government of any other."

I'm always reminded of the extent to which we relied on Christian truth at our founding when I visit the House of Representatives. A beautiful fresco on the upper walls of the chamber itself contains portraits of history's great lawmakers. Standing at the speaker's desk and looking straight ahead over the main entrance, one's eyes meet the piercing eyes of the first figure in the series: Moses, the one who recorded the law from the original Lawgiver. What greater witness could there be to the Judeo-Christian heritage that John Adams was counting on?

Q 88: *Should we allow Nativity scenes and other religious symbols on public property? What types of religious expression should be allowed in public places?*

The First Amendment has been widely misinterpreted in our day as forbidding religious expression in public places. (See the previous question about the separation of church and state.)

Public expressions of religious belief play a vital role in maintaining public awareness that a power greater than the state exists. Maintaining proper separation of the spheres of church and state should never be taken as a warrant to keep religious influence out of public life.

Consider an example from another country. When the communist tyrants held power in Poland, they ordered all crosses removed from classroom walls, factories, hospitals—all public institutions. But the Polish people rose up in a great wave of protest, and all across the land, government officials backed down.

Yet in one small town, officials were determined to prevail. They insisted on taking down the crosses hanging in school classrooms. Students responded by staging a sit-in. Heavily armed riot police chased them out.

Then the students—nearly three thousand of them—carried the crosses to a nearby church to pray. The police surrounded the church. Violence was averted only when photographs of the confrontation were flashed around the globe, sparking widespread protest.

Compare that story to events in our own country. In 1963 the Supreme Court banned prayer from public schools. Many people took the decision as a signal that religion was no longer welcome in public places.

One small Illinois town, Zion, was enmeshed in lawsuits for years. Zion was founded at the turn of the century as a religious community.

Streets still bear names like Ezekiel, Gideon, Galilee. The city seal bears a cross along with other Christian symbols.

I should say, it *used* to bear a cross. The seal came under the scrutiny of a group called American Atheists. Their Illinois director took the city of Zion to court, demanding that the seal be purged of its cross. After years of court battles, the American Atheists finally won. The crosses are now being removed from city stationery and police cruisers.

The courts say the state must maintain strict neutrality toward religion. But removing religious symbols from public places is not neutrality. On the contrary, it sends a highly negative message—that religion is something shameful, embarrassing, or at best strictly private.

As Yale professor Stephen Carter says in his book *The Culture of Disbelief,* religion is acceptable to America's intellectual elites as long as it's treated as a private hobby, like building model airplanes. But if religious believers bring their moral concerns into the public arena, that's ruled out-of-bounds. A Freedom Forum study on religion and the news media found that some TV reporters and producers define church-state separation to mean that "religious dealings in moral-political issues are inappropriate subjects in the news."

What an astonishing misconception of the First Amendment. Your teenagers need to study more about the history of our founding as a nation and be equipped to defend the vital role Christianity has played in our nation's history. Religious liberty is under attack, and your teenagers are on the front lines.

In a school district near where I live, the school board recently proposed new antidiscrimination regulations. These were to include prohibitions against discrimination because of sexual orientation. During the debate that predictably followed, school board members said this would mean that Christian students could not publicly say in their school that they considered homosexuality a sin, that even to say that would be discrimination.

I'm happy to report that Christian students, parents, and even teachers articulated their case powerfully and successfully. They argued that to discriminate—to harass a group or to refuse them equal privileges—would, of course, be discrimination. But to declare a moral judgment that flows from one's deepest held convictions, in this case one's religious beliefs, can never be suppressed. That's not preventing discrimination, that's censorship. Schools or other public institutions become totalitarian dictators when they attempt to restrict freedom of conscience, and this is precisely the thing our Founders were most concerned to guard against.

When that liberty is taken away, then everyone's liberty—including the liberty of the gay students the school board sought to protect—is imperiled.

Certainly no power to prescribe any religious exercise, or to assume authority in religious discipline, has been delegated to the general [federal] government.

Thomas Jefferson, in a letter to Samuel Miller

Q 89: *If laws can't make people good, why do we try to legislate morality?*

First, law is a moral teacher—an enduring standard by which we cultivate order and civility in society. In the biblical perspective, the law is meant to embody objective standards based on divine prescriptions for social order.

We often hear that we cannot legislate morality, but that is not true. When we enact laws against murder, we are making a moral judgment. In fact, if you think about it, the very act of passing a law almost always involves making a moral judgment; we consider some behavior to be acceptable, other behavior not acceptable, and the law reflects that.

This was certainly true in the Old Testament. God gave the Israelites the Ten Commandments (all with moral implications), and God's law flowed from this not only into Israel but also into the whole of

Western civilization. (Even Hindus believe the Ten Commandments are a good, moral formulation.)

Second, a system of objective law, which reflects a society's moral consensus, is essential for maintaining order in society. Think of traffic laws as a simple example. When we enter an intersection, we want to know that all of the other drivers are going to follow the same rules we are. Our confidence is not a matter of emotion; it isn't a matter of whether or not we believe the other drivers like us. Our confidence is based on a certain knowledge that the other drivers are going to obey the same traffic laws. If that were not so, our streets would quickly degenerate into chaos. The same is true for society as a whole.

> *To their discredit, Western societies, long elevated above paganism by the vitality of revealed religion, are today crumbling through their defection from the Judeo-Christian heritage. The loss of that inheritance has accommodated levels of brutality and vice reminiscent of barbarian heathen societies in the pre-Christian era.*

Carl F. H. Henry, "Natural Law and a Nihilistic Culture"

So the law is meant to be both a moral teacher and a means of maintaining order.

Still some people question the law's moral purpose, asking, for example, whether we should legalize drugs. They argue that this would eliminate so much crime that is related to the drug trade.

But this would be tantamount to society's saying that drug use is all right, that we find no moral objections to it. To take away the law takes away the moral condemnation that the law reflects: that drug use and other publicly destructive vices are morally objectionable.

In addition, legalizing drugs wouldn't work. Just visit Needle Park in Zurich, where drug addicts come to get their government drugs, or see what is happening in the Netherlands, where drug use has been legalized. Making drugs legal doesn't decrease drug use; it increases it. And society decays in the process. Moreover, so-called legalization does not eliminate criminal activity because drugs are still regulated by the state; and certain groups, like young people, for example, are prohibited from using them. The black markets and crime associated with drug use remain.

Q 90: *Does a leader's private morality have anything to do with his or her public life?*

For years, secularists have said no. But when a person regularly lives a certain way and makes certain choices, over time that influences the way he or she thinks about issues.

Consider a historical example: the life of Jean-Jacques Rousseau, the famous French philosopher. In 1762 Rousseau wrote the classic treatise on freedom, *The Social Contract*. But the freedom Rousseau envisioned wasn't freedom from state tyranny; it was freedom from personal obligations: family, church, and the workplace. We can escape the claims made by these groups, Rousseau wrote, by transferring complete loyalty to the state. In his words, we become "independent of all [our] fellow citizens" only by becoming completely "dependent on the republic."

At the time Rousseau was writing *The Social Contract,* he was struggling with a great moral dilemma. He had taken a mistress, a servant girl named Thérèse. When Thérèse had a baby, Rousseau was, in his own words, "thrown into the greatest embarrassment." He wanted to be received into Parisian high society, and an illegitimate child—by a servant girl!—would be an awkward encumbrance.

So a few days later a tiny blanketed bundle was left on the steps of the local orphanage. Over the years, four additional children born to Thérèse and Jean-Jacques appeared on the orphanage steps. Historical records show that most of the babies in that orphanage died; the few survivors became beggars. Rousseau knew that, and several of his books and letters reveal desperate attempts to justify his actions.

In later writings he recommended that responsibility for educating children be taken away from parents and given to the state. In fact, his ideal state was one where impersonal institutions liberate citizens from all personal obligations.

Now here was a man who himself had turned to a state institution for relief from personal obligations. Were his own choices affecting his political theory? Is there connection between Rousseau the man and Rousseau the political theorist? In politics and in every other subject, ideas do not arise from the intellect alone but from the whole personality. They reflect our hopes and fears, longings and regrets. The fact is, character is indivisible.

Most of the tyrants of the modern world have knelt at the altar of Rousseau, from the leaders of the French Revolution to Hitler, Marx, and Lenin. So can we really say private behavior has nothing to do with public policy? Just ask the survivors of Hitler's concentration camps.

On the other hand, consider the following story of George Washington (adapted from William Bennett's book *Our Sacred Honor*), which is a positive example of how character and leadership are inseparable.

It was 1783, and the Revolutionary War had just ended. Many of the officers in the Continental Army had fought for years without pay. Rumor had it that the Continental Congress planned to disband the army and renege on its debt to the veterans.

As the weeks passed, the mood of the soldiers grew ugly. Finally some of the officers issued an ultimatum: If they were not paid, they were prepared to march on Congress and seize control of the government.

To head off the crisis, General Washington addressed the soldiers in a makeshift chapel in Newburgh, New York. Washington counseled patience and reminded the men that he, too, had served without pay. He urged them "not to take any measures which, viewed in the calm light of reason, will . . . sully the glory you have hitherto maintained."

The men continued to glare angrily at the general. Washington then began reading a letter from a congressman. But as he read, he stumbled over the words and finally had to stop.

Washington reached into his pocket and pulled out something his men had never before seen, a pair of spectacles. He begged their indulgence, saying, "Gentlemen, you must pardon me. I have grown gray in your service and now find myself going blind."

These words of humility instantly dissolved the hostile mood. The soldiers began to weep. After Washington left, they agreed to give Congress more time. Thomas Jefferson later remarked that "the moderation and virtue of a single [man] probably prevented this Revolution from being closed, as most others have been, by a subversion of that liberty it was intended to establish."

What the Founders understood is that character is the first requirement of leadership. It was Washington's character that earned the admiration and trust of the mutinous officers. His humility, coupled with a reminder of the price he himself had paid for his service, drove his men on to greater sacrifice.

Q 91: *When I reach eighteen, why should I bother to vote?*

Our first civic duty is to vote. If you don't vote, you are abandoning the biblical obligation to be a responsible citizen.

A lot of people aren't voting these days because they've become cynical, thinking all politicians are corrupt. But this is wrong. Most of the legislators and governors I know are decent, honest people, and many truly love the Lord.

Whether you choose to vote as a Democrat, Republican, or for a third party, you should look at one overriding criterion in candidates: character. Look for men and women who will stand up for righteousness, who will defend the helpless, especially the unborn. Men and women who will act with virtue and nobility, who will refuse to sell out their office for a mess of political porridge.

America is a republic, not a pure democracy. In a republic we are to elect representatives who will rise above the passions of the moment. They are to be men and women of character and virtue, men and women who will act responsibly and even nobly as they carry out the best interests of the people.

Because I am a convicted felon, I cannot vote. Take it from me, all you have to do is lose the right to vote once, and you would never again find any excuse for not going into the voting booth.

We must never give up on the political process. America remains the greatest and most noble experiment in ordered liberty. If we lose it, it will be because we simply don't care enough to do what we ought to do as citizens.

Q 92: *Why are Christians always so set on vengeance? "Lock them up" seems to be their answer to everything. Isn't there a better approach to justice?*

Christians rightly insist on government's duty to protect its citizens from criminals, but a teenager asking this question has intuited something important. The "lock them up" approach isn't fully biblical, and, not surprisingly, it doesn't work that well. America incarcerates a greater percentage of its population than any other Western nation, and we still have a society rife with violence. The Bible teaches that our response to crime should be restorative justice, not vengeance and fear.

I can best illustrate what restorative justice means with a case history.

A nineteen-year-old man stood nervously in a Houston courtroom, waiting to hear his sentence. He had been found guilty of stealing his grandmother's car and wrecking it.

The sentence turned out to be simple but eloquent. State District Judge Ted Poe took the keys to the young man's own car—a purple Trans Am—and handed them over to the grandmother. Until the grandmother's own car could be repaired, she would have the use of her grandson's car.

The outraged defendant turned to his lawyer and demanded, "Can he do that?"

Yes, Judge Poe can do that. And his sentence is a superb example of how judges can put biblical ideals of justice into action.

This is not the first example of Judge Poe's creative—you might even say poetic—justice. Instead of sending a wife beater to prison, he recently sent him to the steps of city hall. There he was required to confess his crime and apologize to his wife—in front of a crowd and TV cameras.

In another case Judge Poe ordered a shoplifter to spend seven days standing in front of a K-Mart and to wear a sandwich board that read I Stole from This Store.

In a case involving a drunk driver who struck and killed two people, Judge Poe sent the offender to prison for twenty years and ordered that photos of the two victims be hung in the man's prison cell.

Some critics have grumbled about Judge Poe's sentences, calling them cruel and unconstitutional. But Judge Poe says his ideas come straight from the Bible. In the book of Numbers we read that if one man wrongs another, he is to confess his sin. The book of Numbers also requires an offender to make full *restitution* to his victim.

Then there's the biblical concept of restoration. As Poe put it, "Jewish and Christian law teaches that if you do a crime, you get right with the victim."

The biblical principles that Poe is working from are summed up in the biblical concept of *shalom*—a term commonly translated as "peace." But it means more than that; it means the existence of right relationships, harmony, and wholeness. When offenders commit crimes, they're not only breaking a law but also violating the *shalom* of the community. Restoring *shalom* requires confession, restitution, and reconciliation.

So when Judge Poe forces wife beaters to apologize publicly to their spouses, he's helping restore the *shalom* between husbands and wives. When he requires thieves to confess their crimes in public or when he shows drunk drivers pictures of their victims, he's helping offenders understand the damage they've done to the *shalom* of the community.

And the facts show that Judge Poe's approach works: His court has the lowest recidivism (relapse into criminal behavior) rate in the country, and he says he's never seen the same criminal before his bench twice. Houston voters apparently like Poe's tactics as well: they've reelected him three times.

So when your teenager questions the "lock them up" mentality, tell him or her about the Texas judge and his poetic justice: the judge who uses biblical principles to create punishments that really fit the crime—and that restore the *shalom* of the community. Restorative justice is the truly biblical approach. (Your teenager and you can find out far more about restorative justice through materials offered by Prison Fellowship. See our address on page 210.)

> **[The Christian's] duty of obedience is binding on him until government directly compels him to offend against the divine commandment, that is to say, until government openly denies its divine commission and thereby forfeits its claim. In cases of doubt obedience is required. . . . If government violates or exceeds its commission at any point . . . then at this point, indeed, obedience is to be refused, for conscience's sake, for the Lord's sake.**
>
> Dietrich Bonhoeffer, *Ethics*

Q 93: *How should we live under a government whose policies we sharply disagree with?*

If we turn to Scripture, the answer is surprisingly simple: We live the same way we do under a government we agree with.

In 1 Timothy 2, Christians are commanded to pray for those who exercise civil authority over us. Why is prayer so crucial? Because, as Paul says in Romans 13, government officials are God's servants to preserve order and administer justice in the public arena. Notice that Paul doesn't limit his description to good rulers only; in fact, he penned these words during the reign of Nero, one of the bloodiest of the Roman emperors.

Whether our rulers are good or bad, whether we agree or disagree with their policies, our duty remains the same: to respect and pray for them. This doesn't preclude criticizing their policies, of course, but even criticism should flow from an attitude of prayer. This doesn't preclude disobeying the powers that be, but we must do that only when our ability to obey God is at stake. The example of Daniel and his three friends and of the apostles in Acts 4 indicates that civil disobedience must be taken whenever civil magistrates have resolved to frustrate our ability to obey God. However, when we take this course, we must do so peaceably, without resorting to violence, and we must be prepared to bear the consequences that a wicked magistrate will mete out against us.

In the story we told earlier about Dietrich Bonhoeffer, you will note that he resisted the government. In fact, he joined with members of the Confessing Church (the Orthodox believers) to issue the Barmen Declaration, which officially declared that true believers must separate from the government and from the rest of the church that failed to resist. Clearly there are cases when Christians must stand against an unjust regime that has violated the trust God has put in it. God indeed ordains leaders (Rom. 13), but they must act within the proper scope of the authority God gives them. When they repress religious freedom or when they slaughter innocent people, then they are violating God's trust; they are failing to carry out their biblically ordained responsibility to preserve order and to promote justice. So they no longer are entitled to our allegiance.

But on the whole, Christians are called to see government as God's agent for order, peace, and righteousness in society, and they are to pray for, support, and work with government to those ends.

Key Points in Brief

✓ Rather than call America a "Christian nation," it's more accurate to say that America is a nation profoundly influenced by Christian principles.

✓ The notion of equality comes from the idea that God gives every person certain rights just by virtue of his or her personhood.

✓ The rule of law has its roots in the Old Testament and our theological understanding that God reigns over all men and women.

✓ Christians believe in the separation of church and state. Entanglement of the church in state affairs is disastrous to the gospel.

✓ Separation of church and state has, however, been used falsely to exclude people of faith and their ideas from public forums. The establishment clause of the First Amendment to the Constitution was meant only to prohibit Congress from preferring one religion over another and intervening in the states' rights to establish individual state churches—a practice that continued into the 1830s.

✓ It's vital that the state allow religious symbols in public spaces because such "speech" reminds us that God rules over the state.

✓ Almost every law "legislates morality." The law is a moral teacher as well as a means of maintaining order.

✓ A leader's consistent private choices inevitably influence his or her public decisions.

✓ Voting is a primary means by which citizens fulfill the biblical obligation to be good citizens. It is also a tremendous privilege.

✓ The Bible teaches restorative justice, in which offenders admit their faults and make restitution, restoring the *shalom,* the right relations, of the community. The Bible does not foster a "lock them up" mentality.

✓ We are always to obey our governments, except when such obedience to government would *directly* violate God's law. Then we must obey God rather than people.

CHAPTER 12

How Can I Be Confident about My Future?
Work, Career, and Success

Q 94: *Besides the money, what's so important about work?*

The best way to answer that question is to review the ways in which Christians, following the example of their Lord, have always embraced the dignity of work.

Second-century Christian apologist Justin Martyr said that during his lifetime it was still common to see Galilean farmers using plows made by the carpenter Jesus of Nazareth.

Think about it: The second Person of the triune Godhead spent much of his earthly life working in a woodshop. By that act alone God forever established the significance of *our* work in this world.

In *The Call,* theologian Os Guinness reminds us that even the humblest work is important if we do it for God. "How intriguing," he says, "to think of Jesus' plow rather than His Cross—to wonder what it was that made His plows and yokes last and stand out." Clearly they must have been very well made if they were still in use in the second century.

So Christianity began as a workingman's faith. The followers Jesus drew were working people who rose before dawn to drag smelly fishing nets through the Sea of Galilee to earn a living.

The early Christians were also working-class people who, raised in the Judaic tradition, abhorred idleness and made work a requirement of the early church. The apostle Paul, a rabbinical scholar, paid his own way by making tents. He wrote, "Whoever does not work should not eat" (2 Thess. 3:10, NLT). And those who did work were to share the results of their labor with the needy.

The early Christians did not share the ancient Greeks' prejudice against physical labor. Plato and Aristotle believed that the majority of men should do the heavy lifting so that the minority, like themselves, might engage in higher pursuits, such as art, philosophy, and politics.

Historian Kenneth Scott Latourette writes that "Christianity undercut slavery by giving dignity to work, no matter how seemingly menial that might be. Traditionally, labor which might be performed by slaves was despised as degrading to the freeman. But Christian teachers said that all should work and that labor should be done as to God and in the sight of God. Work became a Christian duty."

When the barbarian hordes overran Western civilization, the monastic communities to which Christianity retreated preserved this high view of work. The industrious monks built enclaves of industry, learning, scholarship, and beauty. They drained the swamps, built bridges and roads, and invented laborsaving devices. They copied the sacred writings, produced works of art in illuminated manuscripts, and kept faith and scholarship alive. In each of these pursuits they heeded Augustine's exhortation that *laborare est orare,* "to work is to pray."

During the Middle Ages, however, the old Greek dualism began to creep back into Christian thinking. Monastic orders began dividing themselves into lay brothers, who did manual labor, and those who pursued the higher, or intellectual, tasks.

Then one man, Martin Luther, shook the ethos of the Middle Ages to its very foundations. Most make the mistake of seeing the Reformation strictly in theological terms. But the consequences in the political, social, and economic realms have been equally profound.

The Reformation struck at the dualistic view of work. Just as the Reformers saw the church as being composed of all the people of God, not just the clergy, they also saw all work—sacred and secular, intellectual and manual—as a way of serving God.

The work of monks and priests, wrote Luther, "in God's sight are in no way whatever superior to the works of a farmer laboring in the field, or of a woman looking after her home." The view that scrubbing floors held as much dignity as occupying the pulpit democratized the work ethic.

> ### *The entire world [is] full of service to God. Not only the churches but also the home, the kitchen, the cellar, the workshop, and the field of the townsfolk and farmers.*
>
> Martin Luther, quoted in *Work and Leisure*

To the Reformers, what mattered was that all people understood their unique calling or vocation; in that way they collaborated with God in the grand design of the universe, working for his glory, the common good, and their own fulfillment.

Likewise, the American Puritans viewed work as stewardship to God, which made their primary reward spiritual and moral. As Puritan Richard Baxter wrote, "Choose not that [employment] in which you may be most rich or honorable in the world, but that in which you may do most good, and best escape sinning."

Christians see work as a means of serving God and a way, along with prayer, of becoming more and more conformed to the image of God in which we are made. That's why it's such a big deal; it's part and parcel of the spiritual life. When we do good work and offer it up to God, we praise God in a way that pleases him.

Q 95: *But so much of work is boring. Does it always have to be that way?*

When God calls us to some task—even if it's something the world sees as lowly—he invests that task with what Os Guinness calls "the splendor of the ordinary."

"Drudgery done for ourselves or for other human audiences will always be drudgery," he writes in *The Call,* but "drudgery done for God is lifted and changed."

Accepting drudgery is one of the ways we practice discipleship—learning to offer up those tasks to God. "We look for the big things to do—[but] Jesus took a towel and washed the disciples' feet," writes Guinness. "We like to speak and act out of the rare moments of inspiration—[but] he requires our obedience in the routine, the unseen, and the thankless." We, his followers, must be willing to take on the humble and thankless tasks as well—and not become impatient with changing diapers, doing homework, or taking out the trash.

The Shakers, a Christian sect that began in the eighteenth century, exemplified this humility. They made simple furniture as a means of glorifying God. They gave the same attention to the smallest detail as they did to the overall design. It was said that every Shaker chair was made fit for an angel to sit on.

This sense of calling helps us focus our attention on God's presence in his creation. Paraphrasing the words of C. S. Lewis in *Letters to Malcolm: Chiefly on Prayer,* Guinness talks of his experience of God's creation "in all its ordinariness, everydayness, and homeliness. A row of cabbages, a farmyard cat . . . a single sentence in a book—each can be seen as a tiny revelation of God as Creator."

> *In nothing has the Church so lost Her hold on reality as in Her failure to understand and respect the secular vocation. She has allowed work and religion to become separate departments. She has forgotten that the secular vocation is sacred.*
>
> Dorothy Sayers, *Creed or Chaos?*

If your child thinks that God is calling him or her to engage in menial work, just remember that for a season the One who turned water into wine and raised the dead to life also made wooden plows—and some days the work surely was tedious.

Q 96: *What if I want to be an artist?*

When Christians hear the word *art,* we're liable to think first of the controversies surrounding the National Endowment for the Arts. What a shame. The first thing that ought to come to mind is our own rich artistic heritage.

Consider the seventeenth-century Flemish painter Peter Paul Rubens. Rubens, a devout Catholic, reveled in the color and motion of the physical world and painted things as fleshy and heavy and substantial. It was a way of saying that Christians don't have to be otherworldly—this world is where God dwells, and it carries a weight of spiritual glory. As we've noted, art history books rarely mention an artist's religious motivations, but Christian faith inspired Rubens and most of the other major artists of the Western tradition.

The biblical justification for art is clear: We are called to live out the full image of God in every area of life. When God created the world, he cared enough to make it beautiful. His people ought to value creativity and beauty as well.

Art ought to be one of the forces that heals the imagination; it must say that evil is ugly.

Ernest Hello, quoted in *State of the Arts*

In *State of the Arts,* Gene Edward Veith describes a little-known biblical hero named Bezalel. In Exodus 31 we read that Bezalel directed the construction of the tabernacle, that God equipped him "to make artistic designs for work in gold, silver and bronze." The Lord "filled him with the Spirit of God, with skill, ability and knowledge in all kinds of craftsmanship."

This is a remarkable passage. The Spirit of God equips people not only for spiritual ministry but for artistic work as well. Creating art can be a calling from God.

We Christians are often concerned with "bad art." Well, let's encourage good art. As C. S. Lewis wrote, "If you do not read good books, you will read bad ones. If you reject aesthetic satisfactions, you will fall into sensual satisfactions." Since God created human beings in his image, with imagination and aesthetic sense, they will create culture of one kind or another. The only question is whether it will be a decadent culture or a godly one.

In 1703 Andrew Fletcher wrote, "Give me the making of the songs of a nation, and I care not who makes its laws." He was saying that cultural change precedes political change. I'd be delighted to know that the young generation was full of artists painting, writing, singing—to the glory of God.

Q 97: *What if I want to go into business?*

Great.

With the best of intentions Christian activists have concentrated their efforts solely on the political arena. Literally every political office, from local school-board races to Senate races, has felt the impact of Christian political activism.

Yet Christians are neglecting a key battleground: the private sector—businesses and corporations. In a large and complex society like ours, the decisions that influence our culture don't always come from those in the corridors of legislative power or even from those in the courts. Sometimes they come from a relatively small number of highly placed professionals who often deliberate behind closed doors. Unfortunately, too few Christians have made a priority of pursuing a vocational track that might place them in an IBM conference room or in a production studio in Hollywood.

In an article in *Regeneration Quarterly*, Don Eberly points to the paltry number of evangelicals in publishing, entertainment, secular academia, and the elite professions, as well as in the corporate world.

The result, Eberly says, is that evangelicals remain culturally isolated, often seeking to influence the world from the comfort and safety of their own bunkers. "Cultural recovery," Eberly writes, will begin only "when evangelicals recruit and train individuals to do serious work within the culture-shaping institutions themselves."

We need to encourage young people to consider callings not only in the ministry or in politics but also in business and the professions.

So . . . whatever you do, do it all for the glory of God.

1 Corinthians 10:31

Q 98: *Just because I am a Christian and go into business—or politics or professions—does that mean God has to be a part of it all?*

Let's consider the case of man who lived a "divided life." Aldrich Ames was responsible for the most serious security breach in the history of the CIA. For nine years he fed top military secrets to the KGB, the Soviet secret police. In an interview from his jail cell Ames was asked how he survived the stresses of his double life. How could he sell sensitive state secrets after taking loyalty oaths? How could he turn over the names of U.S. agents to the Soviets, knowing he was sending them to certain death?

Ames's answer is highly revealing: "I tend to put some of these things in separate boxes" in his mind—to "compartment[alize] feelings and thoughts." That way, he added, "I avoided . . . thinking about" those things. In short, Ames survived by putting his life as a CIA operative in one box and his life as a Soviet agent in another box—fragmenting his life and mind into watertight compartments.

The troubling fact is that Ames is not unique. As Francis Schaeffer writes, fragmentation has become the mark of the modern mind. Even Christians compartmentalize their minds: They put their religious beliefs in a little box shut off from the rest of their life. We may be biblical in our spiritual beliefs yet follow unbiblical views in our everyday attitudes and behavior.

For example, pollster George Gallup compiled candid admissions from people who call in sick when they are not, who pad their résumés, who cheat on income taxes. Astonishingly, Gallup reports "little difference in the ethical views and behavior of the churched and the unchurched." Similarly, religion reporter Terry Mattingly cited surveys showing that students at Christian colleges cheat on exams at the same rates as students at secular colleges.

What does all this tell us? That many Christians are guilty of compartmentalizing our life into separate boxes so that our faith never informs our everyday attitudes and opinions. Many of us are as fragmented in our mind as any double agent.

This is not the pattern God wants for our life. The Bible gives a comprehensive view of the world that is meant to integrate all of life. And like Aldrich Ames, spiritual double agents will ultimately be brought to justice.

Q 99: *Not everything is about God, is it?*

An associate of mine was having lunch with a staff person from another Christian ministry when their conversation touched on the subject of recycling programs. My associate commented that Christian ministries should be the first to recycle, but her companion burst out, "What is it with you? Not everything is about God, you know!"

But it is.

According to the Genesis account, God ordered Adam to "cultivate and keep" the Garden. "To cultivate" means to increase creation's bounty, while "to keep" literally means "to guard." Adam was to guard the Garden against anything that might jeopardize its reflection of God's goodness.

The Fall did not negate this mandate. It just made it harder to obey. The curse extended into every arena of life. But so did Christ's redemption.

Eventually, because of Christ's completed work on the cross, God will restore all creation to its former glory. But until Christ returns, Christians must persevere in their role of "cultivating and keeping" the garden of a fallen world.

Even before Christ came, the men and women of the Old Testament understood this. The psalms are filled with King David's exultation over God's rule and his cultivating mandate to us. David's son Solomon understood his father's words: His proverbs touch on everything from child rearing to neighborly relations to work to economic justice to international relations.

Throughout his public ministry Jesus evoked the kingdom mind-set that consciously takes "every thought captive to the obedience of Christ" (2 Cor. 10:5, NASB). Comparing the kingdom of heaven to leaven, Jesus described God's rule as having a transforming effect on everything it touches. And in the parable of the talents he taught that God expects a return on investment from his faithful stewards, who are to bring glory to him as they cultivate and keep what he has entrusted to them.

> *Christ is the center, the ultimate meaning of every entity. To one who knows Him, practically everything can be seen in the light of Christ.*
>
> Gene Edward Veith, *State of the Arts*

The apostles took pains to teach the church not to be conformed to this world but to be transformed by the renewing of the mind, to guard against being taken captive by the empty deceptions and philosophies of the world or by cleverly devised tales, and to seek truth according to Christ (Rom. 12:2; 2 Cor. 10:5; Col. 2:8).

From creation onward God's rule extends to everything. From our bank accounts to our business dealings to our educational curriculum to social-justice issues to environmental concerns to our political choices—everything must reflect the fact that God's righteous rule extends to all of life.

Abraham Kuyper, Dutch pastor and scholar, was one of the great modern exponents of a Christian worldview. "If everything that is, exists for the sake of God, then the whole creation must give glory to

God," he wrote. The Scriptures disclose "not only justification by faith but the very foundation of life and the ordinances that regulate human existence."

Q 100: *How should I measure my success in life?*

Young people are often confused about what success in life really is. Most see it as material achievement. And television and popular culture is filled with messages about the so-called good life, which is always framed in materialistic terms. Prosperity is held out to be the greatest goal of our life.

I know about this. I was caught up in it in my own life. Growing up in very humble circumstances, I believed that if I could achieve power and wealth, I would find fulfillment and contentment. But the more power and success I achieved, the less fulfilled I was. I discovered that the things of this world are empty, that they can never give us meaning or purpose or security.

In fact, I sometimes think that the poor are better off than the rich because they still think money will buy happiness—while the rich know better. The human soul hungers for meaning and purpose, which it can never find in the things of the world.

You need to teach your children that God's economy does not measure success the same way the world does. What God calls us to is *obedience.* When we live his commandments, as I have discovered in my own life, we find true meaning and purpose and fulfillment. We also discover real power, sometimes when we feel the most powerless. The Christian life is a great paradox in that God often does his greatest work through us in our most humble moments.

This paradox came home to me during a trip to Spain. After I spoke in the central prison in Madrid, Prison Fellowship volunteers escorted me to Basida, a community that cares for prison inmates after release. We drove an hour down a dusty, rutted road that ended at a collection of white buildings.

There we were greeted by the cheerful sight of children laughing and playing in the yard. But once I was inside one of the buildings, a chilling contrast confronted me: some forty people with sunken cheeks, sallow skin, dull eyes. These former inmates were AIDS patients, and most sat slumped in their chairs, angry and bitter.

Quickly I composed my thoughts, addressing the patients through an interpreter. As I spoke of God's love and forgiveness, not one set of eyes looked up, not one head nodded. Rarely have I met with such indifference.

Here and there, however, the smiling faces of the volunteers who lived among the patients and cared for them broke through the gloom. In fact, rarely have I met with such radiance, such expressions of love and joy.

During dinner I asked a young woman seated next to me, "How do you do this? It must be tough work."

"It is," she said with a nod. "But it's my calling. Mr. Colson, you gave a wonderful message, and we've tried preaching too. But these patients didn't seem to hear us. That's why we live right here with them—so they'll see God's love through our actions."

She related a tragic story about a woman who died in her arms just two weeks earlier. Then her face brightened as she added, "But the woman accepted Jesus just before she died." This young volunteer was now caring for the deceased woman's children.

Later, outside under the stars, I pondered what I had seen. I wasn't sure if my visit had changed any of the inmates, but I was certain it had changed one person—me. I had clearly witnessed God's power, not in any glittering display but in the gentle, joyful volunteers who revealed the love of Christ shed abroad in their hearts. That is why ministering to the poor and the needy brings us so close to our Lord.

In every way the Christian life is a paradox. I think back on the many achievements in my life: I was the youngest administrative assistant in the United States Senate, graduated from college and law school with academic honors, began a law practice that became large and successful, and then at age thirty-eight occupied the office next to the president of the United States.

Yet the greatest achievements of my life have come not through any of those things I did, impressive though they might have been in the world's eyes. Rather it was in the broken experience of my life that God did his greatest work. I was in prison, helpless, cut off from my family and the outside world; I was in disgrace and uncertain of my future. Everything I ever did in my life had been a success until then. And this was my great defeat.

And yet it was that defeat that God used for his greatest glory. While I was in prison, he prepared me for a ministry that now reaches countless hundreds of thousands around the globe.

He used my defeat, not my successes. He cared about my obedience, not about what I achieved. He used the things in which I could not glory and for which I could take no credit.

What is the great lesson in this? The great lesson is that while we should always do our best to bring glory to God with excellence, what really matters in life is not so much what *we* do. What matters most is what God chooses to do through us. This is why on my desk is a wonderful plaque with one of Mother Teresa's favorite expressions: Faithfulness, Not Success.

Your children and grandchildren need to know that what matters most in their life is their obedience to God. That is success in his eyes.

Key Points in Brief

- ✓ Jesus himself dignified our work by his labor as a carpenter before his public ministry. His first disciples were working-class fishermen, and the early church consisted mostly of workers. Christianity has held physical labor to be of equal value with mental labor as a means of serving God.

- ✓ When we offer our work as service to God, he transforms even our repetitive and boring tasks. Christ's own labors making wooden plows must have contained an element of drudgery.

- ✓ Christians have particularly neglected the arts and the business world as important Christian callings. These are key areas for the reform of society, as much or more so than politics, because culture is the true generating force in society.

✓ True success means faithfulness and obedience. God often uses our greatest failures for his own glory. We are always to do our best but leave the results in God's hands.

A FINAL WORD TO PARENTS

I hope that you have found these questions and answers helpful as you seek to counsel and guide your own children or grandchildren. There is no higher calling than to prepare your children and grand-children to be God's transforming agents in the world.

Remember the commandments: "Do not forget the things your eyes have seen or let them slip from your heart as long as you live. Teach them to your children and to their children after them" (Deut. 4:9). Raise up your children in the ways of the Lord. "Teach them [God's commands] to your children, talking about them when you sit at home and when you walk along the road, when you lie down and when you get up" (Deut. 11:19).

There has never been a time when this is more important, for your children and grandchildren live in a culture that is awash with anti-Christian messages. When I grew up, most of the basic cultural assumptions were shaped by Christian truth. Biblical phrases were common, and even unbelievers used them. But today we live in a post-Christian environment. So the first task is to be certain that your children and grandchildren are equipped to be discerning. You must help them to understand a Christian view of life and reality and how it compares with the prevailing secular mind-set. Only in this way will they be able to see what is wrong with much of what they take in at school, in the popular culture, or in the pressuring taunts of their friends.

But that's only the beginning. You must equip them to be prepared to give a reason for the hope that is within them, as the apostle Peter says, "with gentleness and respect" (1 Pet. 3:15). Your children and grandchildren need to know how to defend Christian truth in the world. They need to be encouraged to stand up for what they know to be right and not be intimidated and cowed by the often bullying secular elites. Your children can be evangelists with their peers, not only sharing the good news about Christ's redemptive grace but also sharing information about Christian truth and how it applies to all of life.

I pray that you will use this book to help equip young people to become lovers and defenders of the truth.

God's blessings on you!

WITH GRATITUDE

I am deeply grateful to all of the Wilberforce Forum team who participate with me in research and in helping me write articles, books, and *BreakPoint* commentaries. As I mentioned earlier, much of what you have read in these pages has come from *BreakPoint* broadcasts or from my published material. This book is an attempt to distill the work of the *BreakPoint* and the Wilberforce teams into a usable format so that you can respond to the questions your kids will raise with you.

I owe a special debt of thanks to Harold Fickett, a superb writer who has collaborated with me on two other books. Harold did much of the selective culling of the work of our team and of my writing, as well as skillfully reshaping the material to make this more teenager-friendly.

I am greatly indebted as well to Kim Robbins, my faithful assistant, who has worked with me for many years. Kim fills the indispensable role of knowing where everything is, and with her encyclopedic memory she fills a vital role not only with this book but also with the Wilberforce Forum and my ministry in general.

Much credit is also due to Evelyn Bence, who has worked as a freelance editor with Prison Fellowship for many years. Evelyn took the final manuscripts that many of us had worked on and, with her silklike touch, smoothed them all out. Evelyn is a wonderfully gentle and capable person to work with.

T. M. Moore, my valued theological counselor, also assisted me throughout this project. T. M. is one of the most gifted minds in the Christian world today. He and I have worked closely together for nearly fifteen years.

Finally, thanks is due to all of those who are part of the Wilberforce writing team and who have contributed material and writing to my work over recent years. That includes Nancy Pearcey, Anne Morse, Roberto Rivera, Eric Metaxas, Douglas Minson, and our most recent staff member and new executive editor of *BreakPoint,* Jim Black.

For a more in-depth treatment of the various questions in this book, I recommend the book that Nancy Pearcey and I coauthored: *How Now Shall We Live?* That book, which I consider to be the most important work I have undertaken in my ministry, deals with virtually every question here in greater depth.

ABOUT THE AUTHOR

Charles W. Colson graduated with honors from Brown University and received his Juris Doctor from George Washington University. From 1969 to 1973 he served as special counsel to President Richard Nixon. In 1974 Colson pleaded guilty to charges related to Watergate and served seven months in a federal prison.

Before going to prison, Charles Colson was converted to Christ, as told in *Born Again*. He has also published *How Now Shall We Live?* (coauthored with Nancy Pearcey), *Life Sentence, Crime and the Responsible Community, Who Speaks for God? Kingdoms in Conflict, Against the Night, Convicted* (with Dan Van Ness), *The God of Stones and Spiders, Why America Doesn't Work* (with Jack Eckerd), *The Body* (with Ellen Vaughn), *A Dance with Deception* (with Nancy Pearcey), *A Dangerous Grace* (with Nancy Pearcey), *Gideon's Torch* (with Ellen Vaughn), *Burden of Truth* (with Anne Morse), and *Loving God*, the book many people consider to be a contemporary classic.

Colson founded Prison Fellowship Ministries (PF), an interdenominational outreach, now active in eighty-eight countries. The world's largest prison ministry, PF manages some fifty thousand active volunteers in the U.S. and tens of thousands more abroad. Ministry volunteers lead more than a thousand ongoing Bible studies for prisoners and conduct nearly two thousand in-prison seminars per year. The ministry organizes major evangelistic outreaches and reaches nearly 500,000 kids at Christmas with gifts and the love of Christ. The ministry also has two subsidiaries: Justice Fellowship, which works for biblically based criminal-justice policies, and Neighbors Who Care, a network of volunteers providing assistance to victims of crime. Also a part of the ministry is the Wilberforce Forum, which provides worldview materials for the Christian community, including Colson's daily radio broadcast, *BreakPoint,* now heard on a thousand outlets.

Colson has received fifteen honorary doctorates and in 1993 was awarded the Templeton Prize, the world's largest cash gift (over $1 million), which is given each year to the one person in the world who has done the most to advance the cause of religion. Colson donated this prize, as he does all speaking fees and royalties, to further the work of PF.

For more information about Prison Fellowship,
write to:
Post Office Box 17500
Washington, D.C. 20041-0500

visit their Web site:
www.prisonfellowship.org

or call:
(730) 478-0100

HOW NOW SHALL WE LIVE? helps Christians make sense of the competing worldviews that clamor for attention and allegiance in a pluralistic society. Pulling no punches, Colson and Pearcey show that all other worldviews fail to meet the test of rational consistency or practical application in the real world. Only the Christian worldview provides a rationally sustainable way to understand the universe. Only the Christian worldview fits the real world and can be lived out consistently in every area of life.

Weaving together engaging stories with penetrating analysis of ideas, *How Now Shall We Live?* helps Christians defend their faith and live out its full implications in every arena—the home, workplace, classroom, courtroom, and public policy. It is a defining book for Christians in the next millennium.

RESOURCES AVAILABLE FROM TYNDALE HOUSE PUBLISHERS THAT SUPPORT THE MESSAGE AND MINISTRY OF *HOW NOW SHALL WE LIVE?*

How Now Shall We Live?: cloth

How Now Shall We Live? Study Guide: paper
Two thirteen-week Bible studies to help people absorb and apply the concepts of Colson's magnum opus.

How Now Shall We Live? Audio Book: The abridged version on four audiocassettes.

Answers to Your Kids' Questions: A guide to help parents know how to talk to their kids about the worldview issues they face every day.

To Be Published Spring 2001

The Student Guide to How Now Shall We Live?
Core truths of *How Now Shall We Live?* presented in an easy-to-read and practical format for both young people and adults.

Complete adult and youth video curriculum is available from LifeWay Church Resources.

Order by writing to LifeWay Church Resources Customer Service, MSN 113; 127 Ninth Avenue North; Nashville, TN 37211-0113; by calling toll free (800) 458-2772; by faxing (615) 251-5933; or by e-mailing customerservice@lifeway.com

LOOK FOR OTHER BOOKS AND MATERIALS BASED ON *HOW NOW SHALL WE LIVE?* FROM TYNDALE HOUSE PUBLISHERS.

Visit these Web sites for more information:

Charles Colson's books and tapes: chuckcolson.com
Breakpoint: breakpoint.org
Prison Fellowship Ministries: pfm.org
Other books by Tyndale House Publishers: tyndale.com

Addresses for more information:

Terry White
Communications Department
Prison Fellowship Ministries
P.O. Box 17500
Washington, DC 20041-0500

Public Relations
Tyndale House Publishers, Inc.
351 Executive Drive
Carol Stream, IL 60188
phone: (800) 323-9400
fax: (630) 668-3245